The
Empathic
Imagination

A NORTON PROFESSIONAL BOOK

The Empathic Imagination

Alfred Margulies, M.D.

W. W. Norton & Company New York London

An earlier version of Chapter 1 entitled "Toward empathy: The uses of wonder" appeared in the *American Journal of Psychiatry, 141,* 1984, pp. 1025–1033.

An earlier version of Chapter 2 entitled "On listening to a dream: The sensory dimensions" appeared in *Psychiatry, 48,* 1985, pp. 371–381.

Published simultaneously in Canada by Penguin Books Canada Ltd., 2801 John Street, Markham, Ontario L3R 1B4.

Printed in the United States of America

Library of Congress Cataloging-in-Publication Data

Margulies, Alfred.
    The empathic imagination / Alfred Margulies. — 1st ed.
        p.   cm.
    "A Norton professional book."
    Bibliography: p.
    Includes index.
    1. Empathy.   2. Psychotherapist and patient.   I.   Title.
RC489.E46M37   1989
616.89'14—dc19   88-37075

ISBN 0-393-70076-3

W. W. Norton & Company, Inc., 500 Fifth Avenue, New York, N. Y. 10110
W. W. Norton & Company Ltd., 37 Great Russell Street, London WC1B 3NU

1 2 3 4 5 6 7 8 9 0

For my wife Bonnie
and my children Lauren and Lisa

and in memory of my parents Sarah and Irving

Contents

The extremest resources of the imagination are called in to lay open the deepest movements of the heart.

—WILLIAM HAZLITT

Preface

*A preface might be called a
lightning conductor.*
—LICHTENBERG
Aphorisms, I, 1775–1779

H istory conferred on James and Alix Strachey the task of making
Freud's complete psychological works available to the English-speak-
ing world. Translation did not always come easily—and the German word
Einfühlung posed particular problems for them. *Einfühlung* has since been
handed down to us as "empathy," a word (I was surprised to learn) relatively
new to the English language and one only listed in the supplement of the
Oxford English Dictionary. In a personal letter to her husband (Jan 2,
1925), Alix wrote:

> By the way, about the word "empathy." Did *I* suggest it? It's only that at a tea-
> party Abraham said that Jones had found or invented this word for "Ein-
> fühlung"; & I had a sort of feeling that Bullough [a former professor of hers] had
> created it, for aesthetic purposes, 11 years ago, & that I picked it up there. In any
> case it's a vile word, elephantine, for a subtle process. I can't help feeling a real
> English writer would at once produce the right word. The process *must* have a
> name. (Strachey and Strachey, 1985, pp. 170–171)

Alix Strachey never had her wish—that vile and elephantine word, empathy,
stuck; to her the German word, *Einfühlung*, literally "in-feeling" or "feeling
into," while inadequate, seemed closer to that subtle process. Moreover, the
very difficulty in translation itself lent *Einfühlung* an air of mystery, convey-
ing its delicate shadings and nuances. Perhaps she feared that in naming the
process, we would concretize and violate it, pretending we understood.

Road Map

In this book I pursue the phenomenology of empathy in everyday clinical practice. The book's narrative structure is that of a personal odyssey through the terrain of the intersubjective, how it is that one person can ever know the mind of another. What now follows is a rough road map of the chapters to come.

We will delve into four broad and contiguous domains. I begin with the uses of wonder as a precondition for the empathic dialogue. The holding of wonder, a searching attitude of simultaneously knowing and not-knowing, of finding pattern and breaking apart, goes against the grain of our organizing mind, but is intrinsic to the creativity of introspection, art, and empathy.

From wonder I move to the nature of interior landscapes, the sensory parameters of personal world views, and the search for the unique essences of another. Invariably, in searching for the other in an active fashion, we come to our own reflection, the fundamental projective nature of empathy, and the dialectical quality of finding and creating meaning.

In the middle of the book there is an extended clinical example that was written in fragments at the time of the treatment itself. I have done this to capture the groping and unfolding quality of clinical work, rather than presenting in the more usual omniscient fashion of our case report tradition, with all the threads coming together in the authority of hindsight (and the privilege of omission).

The fourth section insisted on its existence: Any consideration of empathy and world view must raise the notion of the self, who or what is at the center of world view and introspection. We come to a reconsideration of the repetition compulsion, investigate the interplay of subjective world view and symptom experience, and explore the concept of empathy-with-oneself. Here I examine the parallel and multiple conceptions of the self in clinical work from psychoanalytic to interpersonal to existential points of view and the inherent dilemma for the empathizer of divided states of consciousness.

The quest for empathy leads to the irreducible paradox of the self — which defines and finds itself through the other in its own reflective and interpersonal spiral. Paradox is at the heart of therapeutic work and empathy in particular embodies its irony, subtlety, and wonder. We return to the holding of simultaneously opposing states of mind, the intertwining of subject-object reflections, and the creation of metaphor and meaning in the search for the inner life of another.

Lightning Conductor

The preface is an odd beast: it comes at the beginning of a book — though it is written at the end. I know, in a way the reader can't, what the book has become and what it hasn't. Now that I have finished the journey of the book, the path seems inevitable to me, though this was not always the case. Throughout I have tried to preserve the quality of my reasoning as it unfolded to me, and the larger questions that emerged along the way, things so basic and so difficult that the tendency is to put them aside.

Initially I tried to evolve these ideas through articles submitted to journals. Gradually I came to the realization that such a medium was not conducive to the sustained development of thought. In subsequent papers I could not rely on the reader being familiar with the preceding ones, and so I would have to lay the foundation anew with each communication, cutting into the allotted room of an article and leaving little latitude to advance. It became clear to me that the space of a book was necessary to develop the maturing logic of my reflections. And so I invite you to trace with me my journey toward understanding.

A dialogue with an imagined reader is an elusive thing. You were there with me, hovering over my shoulder as I wrote; I constructed you from my own wishes and fears, memories and hopes, filling the void between us with bits and pieces of my own experience. No doubt you are very different from the person I have imagined, and you will now see things along the way that I did not, coming to your own different and personal conclusions. This is the way it should be: Like psychotherapy, every dialogue — even an imagined one — will be unique and unrepeatable.

The
Empathic
Imagination

PART I
Toward Empathy

Then I felt like some watcher of the skies
When a new planet swims into his ken . . .

—JOHN KEATS

CHAPTER 1

The Uses of Wonder

> *The word "precursor" is*
> *indispensable in the vocabu-*
> *lary of criticism, but one*
> *should try to purify it from*
> *every connotation of*
> *polemic or rivalry. The fact*
> *is that each writer* creates *his*
> *precursors. His work*
> *modifies our conception of*
> *the past, as it will modify the*
> *future.*
> —BORGES (1981, p. 243)

How does one begin to approximate the inner experience of another? This enigmatic process, empathy, approaches to the heart of the workaday world of the therapist, streaming paradox in its wake. The empathic exploration demands of the investigator the creative capacity to suspend closure, to know and not know simultaneously. In this chapter, I will draw on three disparate sources for understanding the mysterious journey to the interior of another: phenomenology, psychoanalysis and poetry—all observational, subjective, and creative endeavors. And though I try to remain true to the intent of the writers who enlighten me, I inevitably invent my predecessors and fashion them to my own purposes.

Drawing parallels between the works of one writer and another becomes a surprising pursuit: The parallels themselves assume a life of their own. One's way of reading changes; familiar words take on new meanings as the context of the reading evolves. Understanding bounces along on a dialectical journey, drawing its energy from contradictions and defining itself by its very movement from one problem to the next.

This study begins with a comparison of two introspective methods of investigation, phenomenology and psychoanalysis. Phenomenology, as that branch of philosophy which is the "study of man's consciously reported experiences" (Freedman, Kaplan, and Sadock, 1975, p. 2599), would seem to complement psychoanalysis and its emphasis on the unconscious. Furthermore, the methods of each school are similar in the spirit of discovery infused into the basic design of their investigatory recommendations. The founders of both schools, Husserl and Freud, took care to provide the researcher with tools that could simultaneously clear the perceptual field and potentiate the acquisition of new data. The investigatory methods, by their very nature, should resist routinization. They are self-renewing for observational novelty.

Experiencing freshly is, in a manner of speaking, a technical concern for artists as well. How can the poet continue to see the world anew and avoid the dangers of observational stagnation, the tyranny of ideas, and the reduction to stereotypes and gimmicks? John Keats, in letters and personal remarks, is especially helpful in this regard. His struggle to articulate the creative process sheds light on the fundamental problem of seeking the reality, the truth, of the other. Keats's search for the internal experience of the other has particular relevance to the psychological investigator and will lead us, at the end of this chapter, to the question of empathy and the creative imagination.

Regarding empathy itself, Freud wrote that it "plays the largest part in our understanding of what is inherently foreign to our ego" (Freud, 1921, p. 108); only through its presumption are we enabled "to take up any attitude at all towards another mental life" (p. 110). But, Freud felt, the process itself remained a neglected and unsolved theoretical problem. Despite the mystery of how it occurs, many clinicians have long assumed that empathy is a basic ingredient of psychotherapeutic work; yet, only relatively recently has empathy received much focus in the literature of psychotherapy, almost as if its importance were being rediscovered. For Kohut empathy became a cornerstone of self psychology: The "idea itself of an inner life of man, and thus of a psychology of complex mental states, is unthinkable, without our ability to know via vicarious introspection—my definition of empathy" (1977, p. 306). Empathy has now moved to the center stage of our theoretical debates as we begin to clarify its complexity as a developmental and therapeutic process.

This leg of my own journey, however, did not start as a study of empathy. Empathy emerged as a surprising consequence of an exploration into the recommendations of three remarkable observers of experience. The path of this chapter, then, begins with phenomenology and a curious similarity to psychoanalysis, moves to Keats and his quest for the "negative capability," and goes on to the nature of the empathic attitude.

Clearing the Perceptual Field

In the history of ideas there is much to being in the right place at the right time. Ellenberger (1958), in his fine summary of psychiatric phenomenology and existential analysis, noted that in several externals Freud's and Husserl's lives coincide. They lived from the 1850s to the late 1930s; they published their principal works, *The Interpretation of Dreams* and *Logical Investigations*, in 1900; and they shared a teacher, Franz Brentano, a philosopher interested in the nature of the mind's constitution of "reality." Ellenberger suggested that Husserl's method of the phenomenological reduction is comparable to Freud's "basic rule" of free association: Both techniques prepare the subject to put aside the usual biases to observation. Both investigators knew that it is in the nature of the mind to resist certain explorations.

But, of course, there were fundamental differences in approach. Though phenomenology was to become a complexly intellectual field with its own forbidding jargon, it originated in reaction to explanatory systems like Freud's. The ideal was a return to the raw data of experience. As Merleau-Ponty, a student of Husserl, put it:

> To turn back to the things themselves is to return to that world prior to knowledge of which knowledge speaks, and with regard to which every scientific determination is abstractive, dependent and a sign; it is like the relationship of geography to the countryside where we first learned what a forest, a prairie or a river was. (1964, p. 84)

For the clinician, one appeal of phenomenology was as a mode of access to the varieties of human experience. What was the world like for the schizophrenic, for the compulsive, for the suicidal? How did time and color change for the depressed or for the murderer? These were worlds heretofore unexplored — even obscured — by the usual scientific approaches which interposed "ideas" about the person. The inner life of the other could easily be lost amidst all the "data."

Ellenberger (1958) described Husserl's method, the phenomenological reduction,[1] as follows:

> In the presence of a phenomenon (whether it be an external object or a state of mind), the phenomenologist uses an absolutely unbiased approach; he observes phenomena as they manifest themselves and only as they manifest themselves. . . .

The observer . . . excludes from his mind not only any judgment of value about the phenomena but also any affirmation whatever concerning their cause and background; he even strives to exclude the distinction of subject and object. . . . With this method, observation is greatly enhanced: the less apparent elements of phenomena manifest themselves with increasing richness and variety, with finer gradations of clarity and obscurity, and eventually previously unnoticed structures of phenomena may become apparent. (p. 96)

Whereas Freud's studies moved to the inner borders of the mind, where consciousness meets unconscious, Husserl moved to the outer edges, where consciousness merges with the realm of the senses. In probing the unconscious, Freud became aware of internal resistances, defense mechanisms that he broadly grouped as "repression." Similarly, in his exploration of consciousness, Husserl directed his rule of reduction to the biases in perception; here Freud would have referred to the broad group of defenses directed against perception, or the denial mechanisms. To paraphrase Merleau-Ponty (1964), the whole effort of phenomenology is to recover a naive contact with the world. How can one approximate the bare and subtle essences of things?

Each school of psychology, of course, captures a different essence of the mind; each attempts to exhaust the possibilities of its primary assumptions about what is important. Havens' (1973) work is invaluable in its exploration of the methods and data of the principal schools of psychiatry. He stresses the intertwining of the method used and the facts secured: The two go firmly hand in hand. Each approach defines and is defined by its field of interest, and each leads to its own brand of "truth."

Phenomenology and existentialism share a common field of concern: the subjective and whole experience of the individual. Existentialism, with its emphasis on a person's unique relationship to freedom, responsibility, and meaning, finds its roots in the phenomenological interest in individual consciousness and world view. Given the existentialists' incorporation of phenomenology, we find that their "facts" merge into a continuum. One such "fact" is the variety of ways in which we refuse to experience the world or ourselves, the self-deception, or denial, of our senses. An analogy to another school of psychiatry might be of help in understanding this process.

It was Havens (personal communication) who first suggested that the existentialists stand in a similar relationship to "denial" as Sullivan and the interpersonalists did to "transference." Harry Stack Sullivan (1954) was interested in how people distort one another, how we bring omnipresent personal stereotypes into our social interactions, ready to spring them on our unsuspecting neighbor. In many ways Sullivan's interest in such distortion was an inevitable outgrowth of Freud's discovery of transference. To his dismay Freud found that patients in analysis regularly experienced him in a manner characteristic of earlier relationships in their lives; Freud's genius was to utilize such transference reactions as a vehicle for the treatment. It was Sullivan's genius that pushed the concept of transference to its limits, extending its implications into everyday life, the idea of parataxic distortions. "Transference" is not limited to the psychiatric consulting room.

In similar fashion the existentialists extended the implications of denial into everyday life. Denial, by definition, is "an unconscious defense mechanism in which an aspect of external reality is rejected" (Freedman, Kaplan, and Sadock, 1975, p. 2582). In other words, the individual unconsciously refuses to acknowledge the *perception* of an external fact that is threatening or painful. Implicit in existential formulations of freedom, responsibility, and death are notions of such defenses. Indeed, the existentialists insist that there are universally denied facts of existence. For example, it is part of the human condition to balk at the thought of one's individual obliteration. We cannot bear it and spend part of our lives denying the inevitability of a personal death. In this sense, denial is omnipresent, just as are parataxic distortions in our interpersonal relationships.

Collective denial states, by their very collective nature, are usually lost to us. It is one thing to shake one's head in understanding another's refusal to face the facts; it is something else to apprehend the denial inherent in culture or common existence. Denial of death is the usual state of affairs for most of us; it seems odd or morbid when a writer dwells on death for too long. Perhaps it is their strong objection to this universal consensual *in*validation of experience by the mass of humanity that gives some existentialists such a strident quality. It is as if they are trying to shake us awake with their insistence on choice, freedom, and, of course, death. And so too we might understand why some of the strongest voices of existentialism have come from those who have lived under extreme circumstances, for example, the Holocaust or near fatal illness. It is the very uncommonness and severity of such life experiences that puncture our everyday complacency and neurotic preoccupations.

The phenomenologists, however, pushed the concept of denial further than the universal denial states. Something akin to denial permeates even our nonemotional perceiving. Our very perceptual apparatus becomes forever enslaved through experiences and "knowing." Phenomenologists were trying for experience straight and without interpretation; phenomenology was to be a descriptive psychology, not an explanatory or "genetic" science (Wyss, 1973). Wordsworth referred to "the meddling intellect": "Knowing" changes our relationship to the universe (Engell, 1981). Once we have learned how a thing is *supposed* to be, we experience it differently—and never again as directly. Maturity places an obscuring veil of understanding between us and the world.

Artists are intuitively aware of such cognitive enslavement. A recent popular book claims to train its readers to "draw with the right side of the brain," the side that does not know in a linear, logical way. We are to perceive intuitively, without thinking about perceiving.[2] Picasso purportedly claimed that it took him just a few years to draw like Raphael, but the rest of his life to learn to paint like a child. Children's eyes are fresh, and "primitive" artists have been valued for their ability to capture the world anew. "Knowing" what an object looks like transmutes into what we actually see.

Husserl's objective was to shake patterned perceptions, to clear habituated vision. Against every tendency to the contrary the phenomenological observer is to push aside all concepts, all knowledge, of the objects observed. Husserl called this attempt to stave off such knowing "putting the world between brackets," an isolating of experience against the intrusions of cognitive distractions (1962). MacLeod described it as "an attitude of disciplined naiveté," the vision of a trained primitive (May, 1969, p. 21). The world was to be "reduced" to pure perception, the "phenomenological reduction." Husserl's rule then was simple and arduous: "In the presence of a phenomenon . . . the phenomenologist uses an absolutely unbiased approach; he observes phenomena as they manifest themselves and only as they manifest themselves" (Ellenberger, 1958, p. 96).

The reader might immediately take exception: This is the "tabula rasa" notion in sheep's clothing. Locke had compared the mind to a clean slate that is written on by experience, a conception of the mind as passively receiving and organizing experience. Husserl seemed to be arguing that even if the mind is not actually a blank slate, the ideal is to behave as if it were—perception is to be divorced from cognition. Many psychological investigators have compellingly challenged such a notion. For example, implicit in Piaget's work on the acquisition of logical processes in children is the interplay of the assimilation of information and the accommodation of the internal structures of mind to new input (1966, 1986). Assimilation and accommodation, perception and cognitive schemata, mold one another: There are no "natural" perceptions apart from the organizing mind. In philosophy, the broad tradition of the constructivists (including Kant, Berkeley, Goodman, Bruner) deals with the nature of the mind's structuring of "external" reality. Karl Popper (1968), too, has made forceful arguments about the organizing quality of mind on perception and on the advancement of scientific knowledge through the framing of falsifiable hypotheses.

Husserl was not so naive as to believe that the phenomenological reduction was even possible. No, it was an ideal, a beacon for the investigator's navigation into uncharted areas. It was Husserl's acute awareness that we, as active participants, *must* always construct a subjective reality (that is, intentionality) that gave rise to his method. He was trying to deconstruct, to take apart bit by bit, the body of one's elaborate contributions to perception, systematically teasing out its component parts. Husserl compared putting the world between brackets to Descartes' "attempt to doubt," even when all of knowledge tells us otherwise about our perceptions. One works at it, identifying the assumptions that influence perception: "That we should set aside all previous habits of thought, see through and break down the mental barriers which these habits have set along the horizons of our thinking . . . these are hard demands . . . to move freely along this new way . . . to learn to see what stands before our eyes, to distinguish, to describe, calls . . . for exacting and laborious studies" (as quoted in Misiak and Sexton, 1973, p. 8).

Perhaps the best one can do is to bracket one hypothesis at a time in the manner of the experimental technique of isolating variables. Merleau-Ponty (1964) wrote of Husserl's injunction, "This reduction is the decision not to suppress but to place in suspense, or out of action, all the spontaneous affirmations in which I live, not to deny them but rather to understand them and to make them explicit" (p. 56). The investigator's struggle must be endless: The greatest teaching of the phenomenological reduction according to Merleau-Ponty is, in fact, its impossibility.

As a first approximation to his new method, Husserl (1962) borrowed Descartes' "attempt to doubt" — but now "only as a device of method" and with a new purpose in mind: "to put out of action" the "fact-world" of obscuring theories. Indeed, unlike Descartes, Husserl was not doubting the world at all, but attempting to return to the realness of experience itself. In this spirit, then, one might attempt to doubt or reduce even the most concrete phenomena, to force the imagination into consideration of what is a priori assumed impossible. As Husserl put it, "The attempt to doubt everything has its place in the realm of our *perfect freedom*. We can *attempt to doubt* anything and everything, however convinced we may be concerning what we doubt, even though the evidence which seals our assurance is completely adequate" (p. 97). One is reminded of Einstein's extraordinary *Gedanken* or thought experiments, flights of the mind contradicting everything known about physical principles.

Perhaps the reader objects to this train of reasoning. Denial is a defense against an affect, a dynamic to prevent pain, but I am stressing perception, a less affective emphasis. It would be wrong to say that perceptual modes, even if inflexible, are an extension of denial in any usual sense of that word.

This is, of course, true — but our semantic divisions lose their clarity around the vexing problems of self-perception. As I will explore in subsequent chapters, one constructs a world view and within this subjectivity perceives the world as if external and given in reality. Moreover, one constructs oneself as both subject and object within one's world view. The therapist's and patient's tasks are ones of creating new possibilities of self from within a given set of world views.

When it comes to the self-objectifying-the-self we are confronted with the problem of perceptual rigidity which has both cognitive and defensive aspects and is of considerable importance to therapists interested in the evolution of self-change. Freud (1940) and Jacobson (1957) discussed the problems of self-fragmentation consequent to the ego's use of the mechanism of denial. Denial sets the feeling-self against the perceiving-self, compartmentalizing awareness and dividing the ego.

I am interested here in the challenges of perceiving freshly and in particular of opportunities for the self to conceive of the self anew: in other words, the therapeutic application of creativity to the image of self, the opening of new possibilities of self-perception. In later chapters I will come back to this paradox of the self-reflective self and of possibilities still nascent and outside the constructed world of what the individual can as yet see or imagine. For now I will turn to Freud and his radical conception of the tool of free association.

Free Association and Evenly Hovering Attention

Freud's method of free association was originally devised for reasons quite different from those underlying the development of the phenomenological reduction. Freud was interested in the tapestry of the unconscious and wanted a method that would expose its threads. Hypnosis, in his hands, proved unreliable and, with his new method, unnecessary. The unconscious would reveal its outlines if patients would say "whatever comes into their heads, even if they think it unimportant or irrelevant or nonsensical . . . not omitting any thought or idea from their story because to relate it would be embarrassing or distressing to them" (1904, p. 251).

This rule, the fundamental rule of psychoanalysis, is also an ideal — virtually impossible. It has been said that when the patient can truly free associate, it is time to terminate. Perhaps most of the work of psychoanalysis is analyzing why the patient cannot freely associate, that is, analyzing the resistances to saying what comes to mind. The patient is to put aside what he or she knows or thinks is important and is to say everything. The ideal is to suspend judgment.

My analogy must now be evident to the reader. In suspending judgment about the contents of the mind, the analysand is being asked to "reduce" him or herself, to put oneself-as-observer-of-oneself "in brackets." The demand of the basic rule of analysis, that of free association, has marked affinities to the phenomenological reduction. One suspends what one knows so that one might discover what one could not see before. Both set the stage for perceiving familiar things in radically new ways; both raise possibilities of new understanding.

Moreover, Freud extended his dictum of free association to the therapist as well. Not only were analysts to train themselves to free associate along with the patient in a state of "evenly hovering attention," but they were to apply an observational attitude remarkably similar to the phenomenological reduction, a stance of not-concluding. Freud offers a striking bit of advice:

> It is not a good thing to work on a case scientifically while treatment is still proceeding — to piece together its structure, to try to foretell its further progress, and to get a picture from time to time of the current state of affairs, as scientific interest would demand. Cases which are devoted from the first to scientific purposes and are treated accordingly suffer in their outcome; while the most successful cases are those in which one proceeds, as it were, without any purpose in view, allows oneself to be taken by surprise by any new turn in them, and always meets them with an open mind, free from any presuppositions. The correct behavior for an analyst lies in swinging over according to need from the one mental attitude to the other, in avoiding speculation or brooding over cases while they are in analysis, and in submitting the material obtained to a synthetic process of thought only after the analysis is concluded. (1912, p. 114)

The analyst is enjoined against any conclusions until after the analysis is over: He or she is to remain of "an open mind, free from any presuppositions." What a succinct summary of Husserl's method! The analyst's attitude is to match closely the patient's rule of free association. As Ricoeur (1970) puts it, "Corresponding to the 'total communication' on the part of the patient is the 'total listening' on the part of the analyst" (p. 409).

We can now describe both free association and the phenomenological reduction in relation to the creative or imaginative. Both processes have as their goal the opening up of possibilities. Both demand the suspension of preconceptions in the service of discovery; such suspension is characteristic of descriptions of the creative process. Further, the processes are unforced and unselfconsciously creative; they are not planned.

Recently a patient was terminating a therapy of several years duration. Reminiscing, he told me that a turning point of his therapy had been the telling of a particular dream; then he recounted the dream with its wonderfully evocative imagery and symbols. These were the last few moments of an intense relationship and the dream once again recaptured the central themes of the patient's life.

With excitement I realized that the dream that he was now vividly recounting was significantly different from the version so clearly related several years before — I had carefully written it down at the time. This new version of the manifest dream was a revised and richer edition. Most importantly, the elements were changed in such a way as to provide new insights not previously apparent to us. His, and my, associations were leading to fresh areas. As the therapy had evolved, our "facts" had evolved too.

My point is this: There was no static truth to be found by our investigation.

The therapeutic truth was a dialectic, a creation of the relationship itself, a continuous coming into being of *possibilities* requiring further exploration. Even our hard won therapeutic facts had been transformed continuously. To use the words of Ricoeur (1970), the analyst "barely keeps ahead of the progress of the subjectivity he is helping in its enterprise of recognition. The phenomenologist and the analyst both realize that dialogue is endless" (p. 388). And he quotes De Waelhans: "From the point of view of analysis, absolute knowledge is meaningless" (p. 388).

Each school must, of course, cultivate the clinical setting for its own unique data. It is my contention that the working methods of phenomenology and psychoanalysis are alike in their relationship to the creative process. They are methods that optimize the potential for novel perceptions and thoughts; they permit the surprise configurations of the new arising from the old.

Perhaps it is this receptivity to surprise that best characterizes the investigatory ideals of both schools; instead of imposing order we clear the field of preconception. In Freud's words about the parallel mental attitude of the therapist to that of the patient, the therapist "allows [himself] to be taken by surprise by any new turn." May's (1958) account of existential encounter is filled with wonder. There is to be an "instantaneous encounter with another person who comes alive to us on a very different level from what we know *about* him." What is sought is "a sudden, sometimes powerful, experience of here-is-a-new-person, an experience that normally carries with it an element of surprise" (p. 37). This element of surprise is at the heart of both the phenomenological reduction and free association—they were methods devised as first steps in the process of discovering unthought-of possibilities. Such receptivity demands a capacity to tolerate uncertainty; here John Keats's reflections are especially pertinent.

The Negative Capability

In a now famous letter to his brothers, Keats wrote that Shakespeare possessed the quality of a *"Negative Capability*, that is when man is capable of being in uncertainties, Mysteries, doubts, without any irritable reaching after fact & reason . . . " (1958, p. 193). How accurately he captured the therapist's and the poet's dilemma! This "irritable reaching" is what Husserl and Freud were warning against; the ability to maintain an evenly hovering attention, to suspend the world, requires a negative capability, the capacity to go against the grain of needing to know.

The organizing, synthetic function of perception is a fundamental feature of the mind. Perhaps this need for completion is built right into our neurological machinery. Kenneth Weiss (unpublished manuscript), wondering about Jungian archetypes and universal symbols, once surveyed the literature on primate "art." Are circles, crosses, and mandalas part of our evolutionary heritage, a primate "collective unconscious"? Would chimpanzees given a chance to work at canvases produce forms of an archetypal nature? Indeed, the chimps closed circles, filled blank spaces, and established symmetries. Whatever the interpretation of the data, they were not random scribblers; they reached for pattern completion and produced a humanly recognizable sense of form and balance. By innate design our egos, minds, and brains organize our experience and establish patterns of perception; Husserl's and Freud's injunctions are counter to this natural synthetic inclination.

The recommendations of Freud and Husserl are comparable to the approach of artists and poets, who first take apart familiar forms, disassembling what we know. As Picasso remarked, "Every act of creation is an act of destruction." Perhaps this is one reason artists have always been feared by society. Certainly totalitarian governments pay attention to what their artists are allowed to explore, lest they destroy the wrong order. The curious psychoanalytic term "regression in the service of the ego" (Kris, 1952) is a semantic attempt to capture such a reversal of the synthetic function of cognition introduced by the imaginative process and the consequent potential for destructiveness. Secondary process with its logical, universal order gives way to the relative anarchy of primary process. To call it "regression," though, seems misleading. Regression reaches to the archaic and non-novel; creativity demands an increase of possibilities, of solutions untried. Surely creativity taps into a nonconscious mode of thinking—but is that regression?

The negation of what is known, the negative capability, topples the familiar and in this sense is an act of will and even aggression. Picasso, as an innovator, established trends in art, simultaneously destroying and building on what had preceded him. Ironically, he set the very context he would work against; in remaining creative, he continuously sacrificed his own work as well, breaking down what he knew and had already accomplished. One price of the continued growth of the creative imagination is an act of self-aggression through negation.

Keats wrote of the poet:

> A Poet is the most unpoetical of any thing in existence; because he has no Identity—he is continually in for—and filling some other Body—The Sun, the Moon, the Sea and Men and Women who are creatures of impulse are poetical and have about them an unchangeable attribute—the poet has none; no identity—he is certainly the most unpoetical of all God's Creatures. . . . he has no self. . . . (1958, p. 387)

On having "no Identity," Rogers (1965) wrote of the therapist as being a "pane of glass," almost not existing. The analytic therapist, too, struggles for neutrality, hoping not to contaminate the treatment by unnecessarily introduc-

ing personal elements. The analyst requires of himself or herself the subjuga-
tion of usual modes of human interaction, an abstinence imposed by the
demands of the method.

This negation of the self by the therapist involves a kind of self-aggression:
to submerge oneself, to submit to not-knowing, and to put oneself aside.
Perhaps it is one component of the sometimes exhausting nature of therapeutic work — the therapist not only bears intense affects but also denies the self in
the pursuit of the other. Keats referred to the obliteration of the self of the
poet:

> When I am in a room with People if I ever am free from speculating on creations
> of my own brain, then not myself goes home to myself: but the identity of every one
> in the room begins to press upon me [so] that I am in a very little time annihilated.
> . . . (in Bate, 1964, pp. 260–261)

One is reminded of Ellenberger's description of the phenomenological reduction in which the phenomenologist "even strives to exclude the distinction of
subject and object" (1958, p. 96).

Both Freud's and Husserl's injunctions are first steps in the creative process
applied to introspection: The therapist and the artist must first permit the
world to be taken apart, living with conceptual fragments and allowing uncertainty, before they can reassemble new structures. Otherwise, "if he follows his
expectations he is in danger of never finding anything but what he already
knows" (Freud, 1912, p. 112). Freud emphasized that psychoanalysis was at
once three things: a method of investigation, a set of theories, and a treatment
(1923a). Perhaps he needed to remind us that the three psychoanalytic identities are not synonymous, or even necessarily compatible. The investigatory
method by its very nature must always be set independently of and, at times,
at odds with what is accepted theoretically. Both Freud and Husserl developed
methods that *should* create a dialectic tension at the very heart of their hard
won systems of knowledge. In the spirit of truth and investigatory honesty,
discord was planted right in. Paradoxically, the more one learns, the more one
must be able to put aside. The very design of these methods, if adhered to,
prepares the observer for the opportunity of perceptual novelty. The methods
are inherently creative and artistic.

Imaginative Empathy and the Inscape

Keats's "negative capability" was a first step toward opening his mind to
new perceptions: "O for a Life of Sensations rather than of Thoughts!" (1958,
p. 185). How like the phenomenologists he sounds: "A point the phenomenologists make consistently, namely, that to know fully *what* we are doing, to feel
it, to experience it all through our being, is much more important than to

know *why*. For, they hold, if we fully know the *what*, the *why* will come along by itself" (May, 1958, p. 83). If only Keats could free himself from what he *knew*, he might experience freshly.

But, there is more, and here W. Jackson Bate's rich exploration of the life and work of Keats (1964) is especially enlightening.[3] Emphasis on the poetic phrase "negative capability" neglects a second stage. Perhaps in some lost letter there exists a term equally lyrical; for now, I must settle for the "positive capability." The German word for such an affirmative process was *Einfühlung*, meaning "in feeling" or "feeling into something" (Engell, 1981; Bate, 1964. The reader will also recall Alix Strachey's vexation in translating that "subtle process"). There was no ready English equivalent during Keats's time; much later *Einfühlung* was inadequately translated as "empathy," which has since become a highly ambiguous and technical word in psychiatry.

Keats's interest in empathy had to do with epistemology. How did the poet come to "know" truth and beauty? Keats was pursuing the goal of *feeling* himself *into* the reality of the other, as if to illuminate the object contemplated from within. The goal of the poetic imagination was to chart the interior terrain, to establish what Gerard Manley Hopkins referred to as the "inscape" (Bate, 1982).[4] A friend described Keats's own sympathetic imagination: "He has affirmed that he can conceive of a billiard Ball that it may have a sense of delight from its own roundness, smoothness . . . volubility & the rapidity of its motion" (letter by Richard Woodhouse, in Keats, 1958, p. 389). Keats (l958) himself once remarked, "If a Sparrow come before my Window I take part in its existince [sic] and pick about the Gravel" (p. 186). Another friend was astonished at the details Keats would notice:

> Nothing seemed to escape him, the song of a bird and the undernote of response from covert or hedge, the rustle of some animal, the changing of the green and brown lights and furtive shadows, the motions of the wind—just how it took certain tall flowers and plants—and the wayfaring of the clouds: even the features and gestures of passing tramps, the colour of one woman's hair, the smile on one child's face, the furtive animalism below the deceptive humanity in many of the vagrants, even the hats, clothes, shoes, wherever these conveyed the remotest hint as to the real self of the wearer. (Bate, 1964, p. 255)

"Inscape," a term that might well have been claimed by the phenomenologists, captures the goal of existential psychotherapeutic work: to enter into and to share the world of the other. The existential worker, like this young poet, strives to live for a moment inside the existence of the other. Rogers (1965) called it "the internal frame of reference."

Elsewhere Havens and I (1981) have written of two broad steps toward the goal of sharing the world of the other. The first step is a proscription: "the setting aside of expectations or presuppositions, the avoidance of concluding about the patient" (p. 423). The second step is empathy, the "imaginative projection of one's own consciousness into another being" (*Webster's New Collegiate Dictionary*, 5th Ed.). The affinities to Keats's poetic and creative process are striking to me. The first step corresponds to the negative capability, the second to *Einfühlung*, or the sympathetic and creative imagination. The goals, too, are parallel: Engell (1981) describes the poet's empathy as dissolving "the boundary between the objective, outside world, and the subjective self. The imagination can, by a process of identification, extend the self out into the world and into other people. The result is neither strictly subjective nor objective, but a fusing of the two" (p. 159).

For Keats the negative capability was a preliminary step to *Einfühlung*. The function of first suspending the self is to clear the perceptual field of those psychic elements in the observer that might impose an a priori structure. Though such a state is actively sought by the poet/clinician and is one that requires a constant vigilance to maintain, of itself the negative capability is merely preparatory, a precondition for the imaginative and empathic process. It is as if one must clean or fine tune the psychic instruments before one can proceed further (Margulies and Havens, 1981).

A hard won insight often seems obvious in retrospect. Why should the creativity implicit in empathy come as a surprise? For many, the literary genius of Shakespeare and Goethe lay in their extraordinary empathic talent. In Keats's time, the critic Hazlitt wrote of Shakespeare:

> He was nothing in himself; but he was all that others were, or that they could become. He not only had in himself the germs of every faculty and feeling, but he could follow them by anticipation, intuitively, into all their conceivable ramifications, through every change of fortune, or conflict of passion, or turn of thought. . . . He had only to think of anything in order to become that thing, with all the circumstances belonging to it. (Bate, 1964, pp. 259–260)

By its very nature, poetic empathy required imaginative and creative gifts. Moreover, though empathy was a talent — to a certain degree one either had it or not — it was one requiring development and training. The artist must work at it.

Yet, in my own training as a therapist, I often felt that, though empathy was vitally important, it seemed a more receptive aspect of therapy, a setting or "holding" function rather than an active, searching, and even imaginative process. Perhaps my misconception followed from the paucity of psychotherapy literature on empathic imagination. Even the current self psychology literature often relegates empathy to a secondary status, a prelude to the real thing, interpretation. Moreover, a genius of empathy in our field, Elvin Semrad, presented himself as a simple man not too interested in big ideas; he was a farm boy from Nebraska. His first-day recommendation to eager beginning residents in psychiatry was startling: Don't bother too much with reading during the first year or two. How well he anticipated that for most of us our problem would not be how much we *knew*, but whether we could stand to *listen*. Though I had no words for it at the time, Semrad had us begin with a negative capability. More often than not, what we thought we knew would only get in the way of our empathy. Our knowledge could be used defensively as protection from what we could not bear ourselves. His very style, though, discouraged identifying with the creative and imaginative aspects of his genius—that was too highfalutin. Rather, we were to learn to sit with our patients, the royal road to empathy.

I experienced Semrad as magical, and, as with all talented artists, he was. Call it *Einfühlung*, empathy, positive capability, humanity, or whatever, Semrad had developed an unusual ability to feel himself into the souls of others. Watching him interview, even at those times when he failed to make contact with the patient, was an opportunity to observe a true creative spirit. No talk was wasted; his words were aphoristic, quotable, and spoken directly to the heart. As Flaubert remarked "Why should the greatest compression of thought always result in a line of poetry?"

Imaginative Empathy in Context

We have traveled from Husserl's phenomenological reduction and Freud's basic rule to Keats and the negative capability. From there the path moved to *Einfühlung* and inscape, or empathy. I have stressed the imaginative and creative aspects of empathy, an area neglected in the literature of psychotherapy.

The focus of this chapter has been on only one facet of empathy, a complex mental and interpersonal process that includes several phenomena under its umbrella. As Buie (1981) has indicated, empathy might be dissected into four components: conceptual empathy (emphasizing a cognitive understanding of the patient), self-experiential empathy (referring to low intensity memories, feelings, and associations experienced by the therapist), imaginative imitation empathy (imagining and imitating in fantasy an ad hoc model of the patient's inner world), and resonant empathy (an affective "contagion"). Buie wisely warns us that such a division is too stark and that in real life there is a blend of these various empathic subtypes. The imaginative imitation empathy, though, is perhaps closest to Keats's idea and the one developed here. Its use involves the greatest stretch of imaginative powers and, as Buie indicates, has a creative quality.

We might also conceptually divide empathy into passive and active modes. "Resonant empathy" and "imaginative empathy" can be contrasted. The word "resonance" derives from the Latin *resonare* or resound. Like an echo "resound" owes its existence to the other: Plucking one string of an instrument creates resonant vibrations in a second. Imaginative empathy, on the other hand, stresses the active, searching quality of entering the other's world: Imagination constructs a new world, one not immediately accessible to the observer. Carl Rogers emphasized the passive and resonant component, the therapist as a pane of glass. Martin Buber, a more active existential worker, exhorted "a bold swinging, demanding the most intensive stirring of one's being, into the life of the other." One is to "imagine the real" of the other, to gain a sense of "the particular real person who confronts me . . . in his wholeness, unity, and uniqueness" (1957, p. 110). A complex empathic stance is at once both a passive, echoing experience and an active imagining of the unknowable of the other. Empathy itself emerges from the ongoing network of these competing and augmenting forces.

When all is said and done, imaginative empathy remains imaginative. Empathy must be checked and rechecked against real experience if one is not to lose one's way and make a fiction of the other. Describing Keats's similar fear, Engell (1981) writes of the "treason of imagination" and the poet's need for continuing self-correction. So, too, the therapist may be projecting his or her own inner experience onto the patient. What may appear as the patient's inscape may reflect more nearly the observer's own internal life.

I have returned full circle to the injunctions of Husserl and Freud. Their guidelines to the negative capability have built-in feedback mechanisms against such biases. One must continue to put oneself aside, attempt to doubt even what seems clear and obvious. There is to remain a constant vigilance to countertransference phenomena in the broadest sense. The therapist must strive for a position of tension between knowing and not-knowing. Empathy is not merely a resonating with the other, but an act of will and creativity. As Hazlitt (Bate, 1964, p. 262) put it, "the extremest resources of the imagination are called in to lay open the deepest movements of the heart."

PART II
Imagining the Inscape

Imagine the real . . .
—MARTIN BUBER

CHAPTER 2

The Sensory Dimensions:
On Listening to a Dream

Try as I like to find the way,
I never can get back by day,
Nor can remember plain
*   and clear*
The curious music that I
*   hear.*
—ROBERT LOUIS STEVENSON
A Child's Garden of Verses

I n searching for distinct inscapes, the dream is a natural starting point. A uniquely individual and idiosyncratic product, it is subjectivity distilled. And so the dream will serve us well in our pursuit of the nature of *Einfühlung,* or how one person feels into the experience of another. In searching for the latent meaning of dreams, therapists often bypass the lived experience of the dreamer and the therapist's own listening and imaginative processes. In Proustian spirit one could focus on the *perceptions* of the dreamer, that is, the sensory world view, an aspect of a person, I am convinced, that is as unique as one's voice or fingerprints. Moreover, the descriptive endeavor itself throws the therapist back onto the listening dialectic that emerges in the ongoing struggle to enter another's reality.

Wonder and the Lived Moment

> to the shore
> Of tangled wonder
> —KEATS, *Endymion*

Any great conceptual tool will inevitably change how we subsequently and forever experience our world. Once having comprehended Freud's discoveries, who can ever recapture the naiveté of unanalyzed experience? I would not be so foolhardy as to put aside what Freud felt was his greatest understanding, the riddle of the dream. But, we might ask, has anything been lost in the wake of his genius? Freud (1900) himself was aware of this:

> I used at one time to find it extraordinarily difficult to accustom readers to the distinction between the manifest content of dreams and the latent dream-thoughts. Again and again arguments and objections would be brought up based upon some uninterpreted dream in the form in which it had been retained in the memory, and the need to interpret it would be ignored. But now that analysts at least have become reconciled to replacing the manifest dream by the meaning revealed by its interpretation, many of them have become guilty of falling into another confusion which they cling to with equal obstinacy. They seek to find the essence of dreams in their latent content and in so doing they overlook the distinction between the latent dream-thoughts and the dream-work. (p. 506)

Freud had the singular advantage of being a pre-Freudian. Like King Midas everything he conceptually touched turned to gold; the landscape he left behind was very different. What we inherited in sophistication, though, we lost in wonder.

Freud's fundamental insight was to delve beneath surfaces. With regard to dreams, the very idea of a latent content assumes that the manifest content is derivative. Our analytic cognitive set is to "see through" the manifest content as not quite the real thing. But the act of seeing through something can render that something not quite real, a shadow or a virtual image without substance. In a word, we fall prey to reductionism, or worse, a not-experiencing. What the patient has lived as very real, for example, a vivid dream in all of its fear, eroticism, joy, sadness, strangeness or wonder, becomes a narrative abstraction to the therapist. An opportunity is missed, an occasion to enter the unique world of another on his or her own unequivocal terms. An ephemeral drama has been constructed for a private theater, and in the very sharing of the dream we are asked to enter.

As with good theater or literature, when we are drawn into the human drama we come to experience familiarity and surprise side by side. Perhaps this paradoxical union of opposing expectations is at the heart of the "aha" or "now I understand" experience of insight: We now know something we already *almost* knew. With surprise our assumptions topple and we discover the other person in a deeper, fuller way. That other great pioneer in dream investigation, Carl Jung (1934), recommended a far-reaching humility in the face of the mystery of the dream: "In dream-analysis we must never forget, even for a moment, that we move on treacherous ground where nothing is certain but uncertainty. If it were not so paradoxical, one would almost like to call out to the dream interpreter: 'Do anything you like, only don't try to understand!'" (p. 96). Jung suggests an attitude reminiscent of the phenomenological reduction: The dream should be regarded by the therapist as "something new, as a source of information about conditions whose nature is unknown to him. . . . It goes without saying that he should give up all his theoretical assumptions and should in every single case be ready to construct a totally new theory of dreams" (1934, p. 95). Jung's advice is not in despair but in wonder; the mystery of the dream presents unknown possibilities.

The possibilities of the sensory inscape were most developed in psychology by the phenomenologists, who reached for wonder. The phenomenologist Von Gebsattel (1938) observed that "psychiatric wonder reaches deeper down than curiosity, interest, or scientific understanding. The wondering has an existential meaning. One wonders not only as a scientist or as a psychiatrist; one wonders much more as a fellow man" (p. 171). One phenomenological method is that of "categorical analysis," in which a system of coordinates of experience is explored to recreate the inner universe (Ellenberger, 1958). This is similar to Piaget's (1954) use of the parameters of space, time, causality, and substance to explore the child's cognitive universe, a way of breaking down the dimensions of lived experience to manageable units of study.[1] Such explorations can be complementary to customary psychodynamic approaches and, indeed, one thesis of this book is that the different schools can enrich one another (Havens, 1973; Gustafson, 1986). The lived experience of the dream is a natural meeting ground and will serve us in the larger quest of understanding the empathic dialectic.

A Clinical Illustration: Imagining the Inscape

THE DREAM STORY

I am in a church, standing with a group of people. (The patient begins his narrative slowly, even serenely, his body still.) My father says, "Look at that ray of light coming into the church. Go stand in it." I go stand in the light.

Suddenly, there is a clap of thunder. (Here, to my surprise, he smacks his hands together loudly—clap!) Dr. Margulies, it was just like that! (His cadence quickens; he is excited and his body animated as he moves to the edge of his seat.) In fact, I actually heard it and woke up—but I kept dreaming, *strange* (said with awe and mystery).

It was very powerful—it was a lightning bolt that hit me. (His voice rises in pitch and strength, quickening with excitement and elation). I start to rise higher and higher in the air and can see the chandeliers. My father says, "Look up." I feel fine, very well, happy.

(Now he drops back in his chair, and his voice ebbs.) But then I get concerned that things will get out of control. I decide to come down, and I do—and my feet firmly hit the ground.

As I listen to him, I am drawn into a vivid, larger-than-life world. It is a religious experience: It occurs the week of Easter, a time of rebirth and, indeed, of the Ascension. What is more, I know this man's wife is recently pregnant. I am struck by the contrast of this intense, dramatic dream and the dreamer: He is ordinarily a subdued man, quiet and thoughtful, and, in his dealings with me, almost obsequious. I am briefly fearful for him. By history only I know he once had a severe manic psychosis.

I note to myself that in its unity this manifest dream expresses a central life's wish and preoccupation of my patient: the desire to rise above his sense of angry, impotent helplessness and his fall from maternal grace to become very special, exceptional. Mother, he has often mournfully related, became bitter and hateful as he grew older. In this session his associations go to his general feeling of being unappreciated and of mother's biting, diminishing sarcasm. He had instinctively turned to father for warmth and understanding.

Associatively he recalls that as a younger man he had found older and supportive men who had been parental and mentoring. With these men he felt himself to be "gifted and extraordinary"—as opposed to the mediocrity and misunderstanding that he experienced in the rest of his relationships. He was at heart a poet who felt troubled by pedestrian, everyday life.

When he first came to me it was out of fear of relapsing into that horror of manic loss of control. He held a conflicted wish for the safe blandness of his daily life, avoiding all strong affect ("Is it me or my illness?"). In his reveries he spun out poetry, often stopping short of putting his words to paper or of completing his fantasies for fear of precipitating some insidious emotional process. He turned to me in an open, polite—even courtly—and idealizing manner, wishing for reassurance about who he was. I felt his longing in his attentive soaking up of my words and his difficulty in ending the sessions, lingering with a just remembered question, a handshake, and then slowing gathering himself together in my waiting room. It was easy for me to understand how the mentoring figures in this man's life would find him appealing and would wish to protect him. It does not escape me that in focusing on his dream here that I too am making him special.

In the following account I *retrospectively* investigate the sensory dimensions of the dream narrative as they evoked themselves in *my* consciousness as I listened. The sympathetic reader will understand that a dream without the dreamer's further associative material and wrenched from a more complete historical and interpersonal (that is, transferential and countertransferential) context must necessarily remain an incomplete account of clinical work.[2] In subsequent chapters I will describe the active exploration of such material within the process of therapy itself. This will necessarily entail a restriction of attention to the few experiential details that it is possible to pursue within the space of a therapeutic encounter. For now, though, the scope can be broadened in systematic fashion to the sensory dimensions of an inscape. In the following example I give free rein to *my* sensory responses to another's dream — the very beginning of my entrance into his dream world. When receptive, I experience a similar frame of mind in the presence of poetry, music or art: Something essential reveals itself.

Sound and Time, Space and Light, Motion and Matter

Let us begin with sound, the most compelling sensory element of this dream. In the hushed church there is a sudden clap of thunder — so loud the patient says he woke up in the dream, though he is not sure. At this point in the narrative, this pensive man suddenly claps his hands — and I, too, am startled. Sound has a palpable presence here. With sight you can close your eyes or turn away, but hearing comes at you. In this case, sound is literally hurled like a lightning bolt. I feel as if he has awakened me from my detached and somnolent listening. With this noise, he jolts me into a more vivid awareness. I have a sudden change in my affective state and with it an excited, higher level of sensory attention. I am acutely in "present-time."

The language used is present tense: The dream is recreated in the telling as if here-and-now. We hear a clap of thunder, see a bolt of lightning, feel ourselves rise into the sky. We are in "roller-coaster time" or even orgasmic time, when everything is focused on the present. There is no past or future — only now, the infinite present, when we fuse with the surrounding world. Sound itself, among all the senses, has a unique relationship to the slippery present: Once one has heard something, it is gone. I wonder if the narcotizing appeal of loud music, for example, resounding music, like rock, is because the transitory paradoxically becomes fixed, it continues to ring in one's ears, "re-sounds," and makes time stand still. Moreover, loud sound is no longer out there — the background envelops us and makes our skin and even our bones vibrate as we fuse with the beating surround. My patient still felt the clap of thunder as he awakened and vividly recalled it to me as if it were still there, thunderous in his ears.

In this dream, time has another, related visage. Experience is sudden and discontinuous; things change without warning: silence to thunder, dark to light, earth to sky. Along with this abruptness, feelings, too, undergo rapid changes from quiet, to fine, to feeling very well, to approaching a culmination, perhaps an ecstasy—but then threateningly things seem near to out of control. (I am reminded of the different stages of mania.) Likewise states of consciousness change abruptly: Was he awake, asleep, awake-in-sleep? Furthermore, like his own experience of mania and like Keats's ode, this confused immediacy of the dream hauntingly lingers long after. It was another existence, in another time and space:

> *Was it a vision, or a waking dream?*
> *Fled is that music:—Do I wake or sleep?*
> *—Ode to a Nightingale*

The lived space of the dream is complex and changing. The peaceful, enclosed, dark womb-space of the church is pierced by light, opened up to heaven, or infinite space. Moreover, the perspectives shift sharply from on the ground, in a group, looking up, to becoming literally on high, expansively surveying those below. The correlative feelings are "inflated" or "puffed up" versus "deflated," and "expansive" as opposed to "constricted"—but now he is also exposed and no longer sheltered. Pursuing a scientific basis of art, the Pointillists identified rules of thumb for visual space: verticals evoke a mood dimension of "up" and "down"; optimism ("things are looking up") versus despair (feeling "down-trodden"). In the dream example, the dreamer literally "gets high" and then "comes down." Minkowski (1970) emphasized the coloring of lived space as well as its verticality (Ellenberger, 1958). In our dream specimen a transition occurs from the darker enclosed space to a clearer, lighter space, toward a mystic space, associated with the "oceanic feeling" described by Freud (1930). The experience of spatial transformation goes hand-in-hand with the internal, emotional transfigurations.

Motion, defining its own properties of space, goes from still and planted, to walking, to rising, to God-like and ascending. Rising, the dreamer feels "very well, happy," but also fearful—a trajectory is implied. Flying, with its panoramic, luminous space, can be powerful and sexual—but one can cockily soar too high, challenge the gods and, like Icarus, crash. Moreover, rapid movement, with its unique relation to the vestibular senses, can be dizzying; space and boundaries can be blurred. As I become confused, it feels as if "things are moving too fast"; the disorienting effect of relativity is felt: Is the movement mine or theirs, inside or out?

In my attempt to describe coordinates of perceptual experience, I am struck by the melding of adjectives across sensory dimensions. "Light," for example, describes not only a visual dimension, brightness, but an aspect of materiality, weight. In terms of mood, both material and visual lightness go together in a kind of linguistic synesthesia or mixing of the senses. If I am happy, then colors seem bright and I feel buoyant; I am "light-hearted," and everything seem to "lighten up." As with other sensory dimensions, materiality or substance can then imply a frame of mind, a pervasive and coherent experience of oneself and the external world, a mode-of-being (Binswanger, 1975). In the dream story presented, the dreamer's physical heaviness changes simultaneously with his affective state: He rises in spirit and then soberly comes down as the gravity of his situation become clear. In addition to setting, expressing, and reflecting a mood, substantiality is also evocative of one's sense of inner coherence: We experience ourselves and one another as "solid" or "scattered"; clinically one person seems "well put together," another "fragmented." Yeats captured the frightening social incoherence of his times with a haunting image of disintegration:

> *Things fall apart; the centre cannot hold;*
> *Mere anarchy is loosed upon the world*
> *— The Second Coming*

In our dream sample, matter itself changes: It transmutes and evaporates. Beginning with his feet planted firmly on the solid earth, the dreamer rises up past the delicate chandelier and then into the ether, without substance. Here he fears things may get out of control, and he needs to return to the stable earth. What a fearful poetic description of the manic experience: It is like degrees of entropy or disorder.

Visual light, too, is an organizing theme and is here pressed into use with a remarkable plasticity. The physiognomy of mood is often painted in terms of dark versus light. Indeed this is one of the more obvious "scientific" principles of the Pointillist movement in modern art: somber moods are set by dark colors, happier by light. After the appearance of the Rolling Stones' angry dirge, "Paint It Black," several suicides were reputedly found with self-blackened faces — the very countenance of despair.

Into the dark stillness of the dream church comes a ray of light from on high. The dreamer moves from relative darkness into the liquid light and is bathed in it, immersed or even anointed. In my mind's eye I imagine other lights in the dream with different textures and materiality, for example, a dancing, glittering chandelier, alive and fragile with its structure fragmented into surfaces. Suddenly, there is the lightning, jarring and jagged, bolting into the clarity, warmth, and serenity of a bathing ray of light. Moreover, the dreamer is struck by lightning; the light is corporealized as an object. Here different sensory modes fuse: sight, sound, and touch come together in a synesthesia. He is literally "thunderstruck."

Synesthesia and Knotted Perceptions

> The eye of man hath not heard, the ear of man
> hath not seen, man's hand is not able to taste,
> his tongue to conceive, nor his heart to report,
> what my dream was.
> —"BOTTOM's DREAM" A Midsummer Night's
>   Dream

Pursuing the sensory experience of dreams, I often find myself puzzled and frustrated by the dream report. I come up against the unknown, the unknowable. There are sensory aspects of a dream that cannot be translated into words. One person says, "I know what I mean, but I can't explain." Another highly verbal patient uncharacteristically resorts to gestures. These are indescribable and uncanny moments in the dream; the person knows the feelings but cannot capture them, let alone translate or communicate them. As a listener I am unable to empathize by reference to my own actual experience.

The unknown and unknowable, like that elusive "curious music" of Stevenson's bedtime poem, Freud (1900) referred to as the "navel" of the dream: "There is often a passage in even the most thoroughly interpreted dream which has to be left obscure . . . a tangle of dream-thoughts which cannot be unravelled. . . . This is the dream's navel, the spot where it reaches down into the unknown" (p. 525).

In the dream illustration the navel occurs at the instance of being struck by thunder and lightning, when sound, light, and touch all cleave together. "I actually heard it and woke up—but I kept dreaming, strange." Later, in retelling the dream, the dreamer finds this moment the most difficult to describe; he is not sure whether the lightning hits him or whether it was the sound, and, when he did awake, he briefly looked for evidence that all had actually happened.

The dream may seem *both* familiar and utterly foreign, a simultaneous déjà and jamais vu. As with the surprise of an exotic cuisine, one tries to distinguish the components, to make sense of the experience, to clarify and recapture it. Part of the déjà-jamais quality is the novelty of unexpected combinations—the dream tears apart the usual wholeness of experience and then rebuilds it into strange configurations. A further contributor to the uncanny is the condensation of different perceptual modes into synesthesias "whereby stimuli from one sense organ are perceived and described in terms of other sense channels, as though short-circuiting processes were at work along unusual transcortical pathways" (Klüver, 1966, p. 6). Not only do ideas become rebus pictures (for example, "getting high") but colors are tasted and sound turns into light.

In exploring the inner workings of the dream, Freud (1900) described the fundamental use of the mechanism of condensation, the "tendency of the dream-work to fuse into a single action all events of interest which occur simultaneously" (p. 179). In the perceptual realm, sensations too can melt into one another like watercolors on wet paper. There can be a blending of sensations into an experience never before felt, leaving the dreamer with an ineffable moment.

Some people with extraordinary mental capacities describe synesthesias. In addition to his astounding memory, the mnemonist studied by Luria (1968) had vividly fused and transposed perceptions:

> When I was about two or three years old I was taught the words of a Hebrew prayer. I didn't understand them, and what happened was that the words settled in my mind as puffs of steam or splashes. . . . Even now I see these puffs or splashes when I hear certain sounds. (p. 22)

"What a crumbly, yellow voice you have," he once told a psychologist (p. 24). In one tone experiment of 100 decibels and 500 cycles per second, he "saw a streak of lightning splitting the heavens in two." Another tone looked like fireworks "with a pink-red hue," had "an ugly taste – rather like that of a briny pickle," and felt "rough and unpleasant" – you "could hurt your hand on this" (p. 23). Highly creative and artistic persons may also spontaneously short-circuit sensory channels. One anecdote has it that Van Gogh, upon hearing a particularly lyrical note of music, cried out, "That's Cadmium Yellow!" – sound had spontaneously painted from the palette in his mind. Some purposely tap into synesthesias through the cultivation of altered states of consciousness, for example with LSD. Moreover, except with flashbacks, these synesthesias remain state-dependent; they are not easily recaptured in memory or described to one who has not had the experience. For most of us, though, the curious music of sensory transpositions occurs only in dreams.

Perhaps such feelings are part of an earlier period in life when sensations were not as clearly demarcated by maturation and acculturation – before we learned how we are supposed to perceive. Recently I had the experience of tasting a strange new candy. I could not identify its taste until I was told it was peach – "Oh, now I can taste it" – and then I *knew* it was peach. In this sense, perception is highly cognition-dependent and clearly related to developmental elaboration and language. As waking adults we can never recapture the unique perceptual reality of the young child. Synesthesias might well belong to a preverbal world or, in William James's description, that time of "buzzing, blooming confusion."[3]

Sheldon Roth, too, has stressed Freud's choice of the term "navel" as symbolic of the dreamer's dip into the preverbal, especially to fusion states with the mother. To quote Roth (personal communication) about the dream sample explored in this chapter, "The navel is the archaeological signpost of the umbilicus, the lifeline to the mother. When one is ripped up and out of this early church-womb, there is sudden light, noise, lack of control, and one is smacked (slapped) to breath — and is never again the same. *Synesthesia* often occurs at the navel, the point of fusion with the mother. The dream then moves up from the deepest unconscious to those states more bearable and more realistic in the experience of the dream, that is to say, more reportable." Otto Rank's *The Trauma of Birth* (1929) comes to mind. My patient, I would remind the reader, has his dream during Easter, a season of birth, and the spring of his wife's pregnancy, her womb showing with his first child.

Sensory Activity and Passivity: The Body, Free Will and Awe

In the dream example, light and sound are dramatis personae, palpable figures on an internal stage — and they have special implications for the human relationships of the dreamer. As Straus (1966) explored, light and sound have different associations to initiative and power, to activity versus passivity. Hearing is a more receptive mode: We "lend an ear." Sight implies activity: We "cast an eye." With vision we can shut out and remain apart; I close my eyes and you are gone — our separateness is exerted through distance. Sound abolishes distance; I am caught by another's voice, and, except by time itself, the sound is irrevocable and can feel overpowering. To quote Straus about "the power of all sound": "One cannot do anything to sound, and yet it is not nothing; it eludes our grasp, we are helplessly exposed to it" (1958, p. 167).

The Sirens' weapon of destruction is song: Ulysses cannot shut them out and must tie himself to the mast if he is to resist the seductive, dreaded music. Only by drowning out the Sirens with his own music can Orpheus save the Argonauts. The psychic representation of destructive internalized objects is often through the medium of sound, for example, the taunting, malevolent voices that torture some schizophrenics who cannot escape their inner noise. In our dream illustration, too, there is a struggle with activity and passivity that is embodied in the senses.

The father initiates and usurps his son's bodily activity: "Look at that ray of light. . . . Go stand in it." With this command visual autonomy and distance are breached; the son does as he is told, passively acquiescing. Standing in the light he is nakedly open to the penetrating scrutiny of some powerful Other. He is the recipient of another's gaze, the one being looked at, but not looking. The son willingly surrenders to something larger. Shortly the light of gaze and scrutiny turns into personified light or lightning, which itself is associated with wonder, destruction, fear and unpredictability. Freud (1916) and Jung (1934) would here remind us of the parallel symbolization: not only the church as feminine, but flying and lightning as phallic.

Moreover, as Sartre (1956) has stressed, the gaze of the other has strong existential meanings. In being the object of another's contemplation, we are no longer the center of the universe. The "look of the other" makes us aware that we can be players in another's script: "My original fall is the existence of the Other. . . . I grasp the Other's look at the very center of my *act* as the solidification and alienation of my own possibilities" (p. 263). The look of the Gorgan Medusa comes to mind, literally the look of stone. The gaze of the other can be in love but also in judgment; as with Cain's mark or Hester Prynne's scarlet letter, sight reveals and one hides in shame. Children's conception of God includes the searching eye in Heaven, knowing all, seeing all.

In his commanding, father is active and even empowering, but he remains the agent of a larger, more powerful force. The feeling is both of attraction and fear—and overall, awe. At the turn of the century one school of aesthetics focused on the real and imagined muscular accommodations one makes in the presence of art or nature. The interest was in the origin and elaboration of certain "total" feelings that pervade some experiences (Langfeld, 1920). For example, raising the eyes and lifting the head in the presence of a mountain create in us an impression of rising, which then animates our feeling about the mountain. No doubt such regular and shared bodily sensations are one basis of idiom and contribute to the empathic richness of language. In this dream example, expressions of mood are suggested by the language of the body. For example, the father commands the son to look up, a prelude to the actual rising and a bodily adjustment associated with awe, that of being "uplifted." The experience of awe, religiosity, and rising is anticipated and begins in the body itself.

The father's command is reminiscent of the biblical story of Abraham's offering up of Isaac and of Christ's sacrifice as well. For a larger good, a son is brought to the altar by a father, and the son accepts the father's command willingly and out of love. Pursuing the logic of the story line of the manifest content, as suggested in the work of Paul Sloane (1979), why does the dreamer first follow the father's advice—and then later reject it? Is it that my patient feels sacrificed for a larger harmony, that father, out of fear or love, did not protect him from the overpowering, oceanic other and that things were permitted to "get out of control"? Or is it that father is trying to liberate him, to sever the tie with mother-church, a freedom that seems too dangerous and at too great a cost? In the thrill of fear and wonder, the dreamer rises; the powerful wish for merger feels both outside and in. Like Ulysses, the seductive pull is mastered only by a great will; he must forcibly restrain himself if he is not to be destroyed by his desire. At the end of the dream, he asserts his own volition, "I decide to come down, and I do," and he regains control — "my feet firmly hit the ground."

The resolution of the dream is with relief, but we are left with a vague air of regret. The ecstatic climax never really occurs; it has been averted and we will never know that other implied possibility of the dream. Nearing the completion of this chapter, I came upon a dream report that surprised me in its similarity. It is in a paper by Jung (1934) and has a less happy ending:

> I am climbing a high mountain, over steep snow-covered slopes. I climb higher and higher, and it is marvellous weather. The higher I climb the better I feel. I think, "If only I could go on climbing like this for ever!" When I reach the summit my happiness and elation are so great that I feel I could mount right up into space. And I discover that I can actually do so: I mount upwards on empty air, and awake in sheer ecstasy. (pp. 98–99)

I could empathize with Jung who, feeling the pull of the dream, becomes alarmed for the dreamer — and even implores him to be careful with his mountaineering pursuits.

> Two months later the first blow fell. When out alone, he was buried by an avalanche, but was dug out in the nick of time by a military patrol that happened to be passing. Three months afterwards the end came. He went on a climb with a younger friend, but without guides. A guide standing below saw him literally step out into the air while descending a rock face. He fell on the head of his friend, who was waiting lower down, and both were dashed to pieces far below. That was *ecstasis* with a vengeance! (p. 99)

Dreams, the Lived Moment, and World View

In saying that many analysts now look for "the essence of dreams in their latent content" and thereby overlook "the distinction between the latent dream-thoughts and the dream-work," Freud is referring to a neglect of the architecture of the dream world. Part of this neglect, of course, derives from Freud himself: He gave us that powerful image of the manifest dream as architectural façade, resembling the exterior of an "Italian church in having no organic relation with the structure lying behind it" (1900, p. 211). The Pantheon is also apt here: plain and unassuming on the outside — but what a magnificent interior awaits those who enter! Freud emphasized the id and the latent content of life; he left it to a later generation to reexamine the ego's contribution.

Jung (1934) took up Freud's metaphor to criticize it: It is a "false belief that the dream is a mere façade concealing the true meaning. [The] so-called façade of most houses is by no means a fake or a deceptive distortion; on the contrary, it follows the plan of the building and often betrays the interior arrangement. . . . What Freud calls the 'dream-façade' is the dream's obscurity, and this is really only a projection of our own lack of understanding. We say that the dream has a false front only because we fail to see into it." Jung then suggests another analogy, that of a text, "that is unintelligible not because it has a façade—a text has no façade—but simply because we cannot read it. We do not have to get behind such a text, but must first learn to read it" (p. 97). Nowadays Jung would refer to hermeneutics.

There is, of course, a larger issue at hand: The dream paradigm has mightily influenced how we listen in psychotherapy, where we place emphasis and meaning, what is considered really real, and what is derivative. Latent and manifest contents, though, have an intimate relationship and are less distinct at their edges than our definitions imply. Following Freud I would propose another architectural metaphor, that of a Gothic cathedral: The façade is the structure. The impressive flying buttresses are not merely ornamental frosting but intrinsic to the support of the building. The foundational elements merge with the exterior design; inside becomes outside, there to see. In Freud's façade metaphor, too, "portions of the interior construction [force] their way through into it at many points" (1900, p. 211).

An objection might be made that this attention to experiential aspects is misguided: it is in the nature of dreams to be perceptually tangled and little significance should be attached to these distortions per se; they are state dependent. It is our legacy from Freud that dreams, though often incomprehensible, are not merely artifacts, epiphenomena of our neurophysiological machinery during sleep. Even sheer manipulation of the brain's cortex, as in Penfield's (1975) striking experiments, yields a personal experience with its own coloring and sense of being. In constituting a dream experience we as dreamers must use our own symbols, history, affects, conflicts, hopes, fears and perceptual modes in a radically individualized fashion—we have no other reality. I can write poetry only in a language that I know and with experience that I can imagine, and I can generate a dream only from who I am. Moreover, in the very telling of a dream I must imprint my unique stamp of narrative.

Dreams, then, are first of all a personal experience and necessarily constructed from a completely subjective vantage point—they are not merely a rebus of symbols awaiting a textual translation in hermeneutic fashion. As with poetry, to understand a lived moment[4] one must first feel into it before taking it apart; otherwise the essence is lost in a lifeless dissection. In addition to sound, light, space, time, motion, kinesthesia, and synesthesia, one could explore many other dimensions (for example, affective states, color, temperature, causality, interpersonal configurations, somatic zones or organ modes [Erikson, 1954]). Each is a thread of a larger three-dimensional tapestry.

A focus on any detail of experience, if explored from an empathic vantage point, must include a full consideration of the larger inscape, which is part of a still larger sense of being-in-the-world. Remarkably and inevitably, a single feature of the inscape, like light, will reflect and articulate in its many different usages and lived nuances a coordinated whole. In the dream example, the internal pull toward the light, or mania, and literally "getting high" is unselfconsciously lived in the metaphors of rising, being light, going into the light, being light-hearted, lightening up, looking up . . . and so on. *Indeed, for the one experiencing these are not metaphors at all; they are the fabric of life itself.*

All of the sensory, lived aspects come together, amplify, resonate, and synergize with one another. These are sensory elements — but not only. They reflect a coherent world view: The inscape is always articulated into the totality of the person. In exploring these primarily perceptual aspects of lived experience through the dream example I am trying to capture the inner world of another. For a moment, I live the near ecstatic experience in all of its vividness; I feel the seductive pull and fear of larger-than-life intensity and euphoria, the connection to the cosmic, the dissolution of boundaries. I can now better understand. This is not a conclusion — no, now I am ready to begin.

CHAPTER 3

Pursuing the Unique

An hour is not merely an hour: it is a vase filled with scents and sounds. . . . What we call reality is a certain relation subsisting between our sensations and our memories . . .

—MARCEL PROUST

Remembered bouquets long since dead . . . left in my memory the bygone charm with which I . . . burdened this new bouquet.

—HENRI MATISSE

One function of art and literature is to communicate those things that would otherwise remain concealed or unknown, to reveal the inchoate idea within the mysterious. Language by its nature generalizes: As soon as I communicate something to you, it is no longer just mine, it is ours. I have moved from the specifics of my solipsism to a more general, speakable experience.

A rose is a rose is a rose; a rose by any other name. . . . Matisse wrote: "Nothing, I think, is more difficult for a true painter than to paint a rose because, before he can do so, he has first to forget all the roses that were ever painted" (Flam, 1978, p. 148). Now I must reverse myself; maybe what art does is to make the known mysterious once again: we must first lose something before we can find it. "Haystack," Monet wondered — and now haystack is infinitely more complex and variable for us all, as it must have been for Monet's own expanding consciousness.

How can I approach the unknowable of the other? How can another help me understand that which has never before been felt in this particular way by anyone else, the unnameable that leaves one locked in one's aloneness?

Case Example: I Am Melting

A young man has the following dream:

> My car is overheating. I take it to a gas station and go into the office. When I come out, the car has melted.

Immediately he thinks of his strange neurological illness. It is a diagnosis made in the past two years and one that has left him grief-stricken and bewildered. He has no obvious illness to an outside observer; acquaintances are surprised when he tells them, since there are no signs. Moreover, he has no words to describe the feelings or physical sensations he has experienced — it is a lonely illness. He has become preoccupied with his body, thinking about it and worrying, observing it closely.

He has always been interested in automobiles and has done maintenance and mechanical repairs on his car. A day residue comes to mind: He had been working on the radiator of his car the day of the dream, the system that keeps his car from overheating. His car has become of even greater importance to him now that he has his illness; he is nearly totally dependent on it to get around. Almost like a prosthesis, the newly important car has to be integrated into his bodily self-image; he broods about it and monitors its vital signs.

When I ask him about the dream experience of the melted car, he observes that the car, though melted, still looked like a car — it was both a car and not a car. This brings to mind his own body: He looks the same to others, but he knows he is not. In the dream he did not feel the heat of the car but observed its effects, wondering whether the heat was dangerous and if the car might explode. He wanted the station attendant to get a fire extinguisher, but then decided that there was no further danger. In his associations he goes to the summer months and the distress they had caused him. The heat had made all of his symptoms worse, bringing out difficulties he had never before experienced.

Initially this man had not come to psychotherapy with his diagnosis, and this is reflected in the dream. He had been complaining of vague symptoms that had seemed chronic and unexceptional to both of us. After noticing his difficulty in crossing his legs, I recommended his seeing a neurologist. In this sense it had been in *my* office that the radiator had burst and the car melted. In addition to linking me to the illness, the dream image provided a deeper, truer sense of this man's horror of what was happening to his sense of self—a new language to approximate that experience-that-has-no-words: a melted car/a melted man.

This was a dream meant to be told to another; it had, as it were, an empathic destiny. We could now, at least, share his aloneness with the unnamable.

That-which-could-not-be-named was for this man his bodily experience of falling apart, dissolving, melting. This now became inextricably a part of his self-image; the most primordial experience of self lives within the body-ego. In the next example too there was a deep sense of an inexorable physical change of the self. To me as outside observer this awareness of bodily transformation seemed symbolic of an even more disturbing and unbearable alteration of interpersonal attachments. But to the person who lived in that inscape it was no symbol; it was real beyond belief.

Case Example: Horror in the Mirror—Becoming One's Inner Image

After his mother came to the hospital asking for help, a 37-year-old man, deemed unable to care for himself, was admitted to the hospital. On an evaluative home visit, the hospital staff had found this man living in squal-or, alone with his dog, trash and filth all around.

I met him in the context of interviewing with medical students. The patient was disheveled and had a fixed delusion: A terrible tragedy had happened, he had turned old over night. When asked about this event he said it was his fault, that several months ago he had started eating fists of pretzels, heavy with salt. One day he noticed salt lines on his chin, like wrinkles. Frantic, he washed his face repeatedly—but to no avail. He applied face cream and the chin wrinkles disappeared, but now he had lines around his eyes. The cream somehow aggravated his condition and more lines appeared—he was turning into an old man before his eyes.

He would peer into the mirror horrified. A membrane had spread under his skin—he was no doctor, it must sound crazy—the membrane then extended from his forehead to his neck, making him very old looking. Again and again he told this story to the staff. How could he convince others of his tragedy?

What would it feel like to turn old overnight? I wondered to myself how old he had felt before all of this had happened. For me it was an imaginative leap into contrasting experiences; I was persisting in hearing his story as symbolic, a kind of psychological metaphor. When I inquired what he had looked like before, he said he had been handsome, and he asked if I would like to see some pictures. They were from college years, and he was indeed very nice-looking. And what a transformation! The contrast of the person in this photograph—a fresh, bright-eyed boy and this stooped, unkempt, and saddened man before me—was hard to conceive, a tragedy of regrets and lost expectations. I commented that he must have had dreams and great hopes for himself at that time. He flew into a rage and left the room.

I thought to myself that I had not well titrated my remarks. I had overwhelmed him. Later, in thinking about the meaning of "titration," I came to another sense of the metaphor. In chemistry labs I had always been fascinated and surprised by actual titrations. One would mix one reagent with another by a very careful drop-by-drop process; this careful procedure, its delicateness, had been my initial meaning. However, at some critical point in titrating, a single drop would convert the color of the mixture—things changed qualitatively and dramatically.[1] I, too, had induced a sudden change in this man's affective state. I assumed that whatever I had touched on had been unbearable. My new image was from Freud: I had hit upon an archaeological find, still intact, preserved by its never having been exposed to the light of day. The very idea of being younger and with those hopes, that future, was too much; it pushed before him the jarring, catastrophic contrast of old and new.

A few days later this man requested that I talk to him again. I learned that he had always been shy, but had once had friends and even a social and sexual life in college. He had given up on that now. In recent years his closest companion was his dog, and so I wondered what his dog was like and asked. Prince was a loving companion who tugged him out into the world—they would walk along the Charles River together and feel a part of life. He took care of the dog and in so doing took better care of himself; life had a pull. Shortly after he had been admitted to the hospital, his mother had had Prince put to sleep, leaving this man in a state of shock, grief-stricken.

Moreover, it seemed as if mother no longer recognized him; he ceased being her little boy. Overnight, it seemed, her affection had disappeared and she no longer wanted to take care of him. Mother had been talking of moving for a while, but he had not fully realized that she was going away without him until the day the movers came. They left only his furniture, Prince, and him in the apartment. "Perhaps," I said, bracing myself for another titration reaction, "you felt your mother wanted to put you to sleep, too."

"I've thought about that a lot. It's called euthanasia, isn't it? I think my mother was right with my dog. Sometimes it makes sense."

He asked how one would go about moving to California, what one does to find an apartment. I commented that it seemed part of a larger question:

How would he take care of himself? He simply had never learned. For the first time he expressed disappointment in his mother—he had never *had* to learn. While alive, father had been overprotective and he, their boy, had always been sheltered.

I remarked that he too quickly had to become a man when he felt unable to, had never felt able to. Abruptly, it seemed, he was no longer the little boy whom his mother would protect. It was, I said, like the story of Rip Van Winkle, as if he were suddenly awakening to find himself an old man. He immediately agreed—but insisted that the tragedy was in his sudden physical change that made him no longer acceptable to his mother.

Focusing on the aging, it seemed, made his mother's decision more tolerable, as if the cause lay somewhere else, in extraordinary bad luck or fate, and outside of their cocoon. Time had fallen on his head like an avalanche, and he had been buried alive.

About two years later I met him again—and now he appeared utterly and fantastically changed, aged by decades. Before he had seemed to me stooped in grief and depression, but now he actually looked to have aged. I asked the new students how old they estimated him to be: They all reckoned about mid-fifties, but not a healthy fifties, that of someone broken by life. And when we talked to him this too was his assessment, that he had put on about 20 years. His story was the same as previously told, only now less frantic. He had accepted the events and lived in sorrow and hopelessness—admitted to the hospital this time because he was suicidal . . .

Pointing to a deep psychological truth—the unbearable grief over a mother's abandonment—this strange story got lived out, concretized in the body. Years later, I think of Hawthorne's "The Great Stoneface," a boy who grows up to look like his fantasied ideal. This, however, was the darker side of becoming of one's internal image. And was it still a delusion? Certainly by any external criteria, his was a crazy story. But now it had become actualized, etched into his flesh.

The concreteness of the body and its position between the self and the outside world make it the most complex object in the inscape: It is inside/outside, both subject and object. This particular positional duality of the body brings about singular amalgams of experience and fused sensations, as with masturbation when the self acts on itself as simultaneous object and subject—perhaps one of the most fundamentally self-recursive phenomena to occur, prior even to self-reflection. (Later I will turn to self-reflexivity as one essence of the self-defining-itself, of bringing itself into being as a unity.)

The next example captures the ineffable experience of the physical condensation of feeling, memory, pleasure, desire, ideals, anxiety . . . all in a single and peculiar body-self sensation.

Case Example: That Indescribable Power

A dream:

> It's night and I am in my bedroom and then I'm climbing out of the window. There's a guard in a car outside the house, and I slip by him, sort of slipping along the ground effortlessly — it's an odd feeling. I then go to a neighbor's house where I call the F.B.I.

Regarding the bodily experience (I ask specifically, it is the navel of the dream) the dreamer finds himself at a loss for words, "It's like those cartoon cats that sneak down steps" — and here he makes his hands twist and turn in right angles as if down some imaginary stairs — "It's liquid and gliding . . . like flying and touching at the same time." The experience, he elaborates, was sexual, fun, exhilarating — and it was powerful, somehow like the "power of skin-on-skin." He thought of masturbating and feeling potent in his fantasies, and how often he feels weak and ineffectual in his outside dealings.

He associated to being an adolescent and sneaking out to see a girl friend at night. That experience, too, felt exciting, dangerous, exhilarating. Interestingly, he could barely recall the actual girl or even getting to her house — the elation of the experience was in slipping away into the night, alone. The peak of the dream was in the indescribable gliding.

Many feelings and sensations were condensed into this difficult-to-describe dream experience. I had not, until then, appreciated his libidinization of danger. On my now asking, he recalled a number of such passionate events in which he placed himself in very real physical danger, even fearing for his death. Later he recalled episodes of voyeuristically stalking a former lover — with the same sense of observing at a distance, hidden and feeling powerful and secretly omniscient, of "being all places at once . . . of knowing everything at once." Here oedipal themes spontaneously emerged, of his secret and dangerous relationships with older, married women and the thrill of pushing things to the edge, perhaps to master, counterphobically, castration anxiety.

Dream synesthesias, the mixing of sensory modalities, often remain obscure — the waking mind of the dreamer protests at the oddness of the experience and tends to dismiss it. In this example, the unique sensations contained a jumble of concerns, each finding expression in the complex somatic dream experience. The sexual gliding, flying, and skin-on-skin, the masturbatory fantasies of omniscient power and perfect control and freedom, the voyeurism and the cathexis of danger were all compressed into a brief moment of tactile, kinesthetic, and sexual merging of dream sensation.

The setting of the sensation also was relevant. It was only much later in the therapy, indeed after he set a termination date (later retracted), that I discovered that he had consciously withheld material that had seemed frightening to him—and that he hoped I would intuit. Unknowingly I had been cast at once in the position of the dream guard that he eludes and of the F.B.I. agents whom he tries to reach, a game of wits and attributed power.

Case Example: Voices to the Right

The physical setting of experience itself, the actual and particular spatial structure of the inscape, often holds hidden significance.[2] This example contains a highly specific instance of a symptom configuration in space.

I had been asked to provide consultation for a psychotic and suicidal adolescent girl. The nature of her diagnosis was puzzling given her unusual hallucinations: She heard her stepfather's voice telling her to kill herself with a knife, but unexpectedly the hallucinations were always to the right and in front of her in space.

So specific a message, so undisguised—did her parents want her dead? And why were the voices so specific in location—was this the recreation of a traumatic episode?

I learned that after years of quiet she had become vociferous about her stepfather's sexual abuse of her. She had been 12 at the time, had loved him, and felt terribly torn and betrayed. Her mother did not want to hear this, and the daughter had been extruded from their home, which was in another state. They now wanted her out of their lives.

I asked specifically about the experience of her hallucinations.

When she heard voices, she said, she also saw her stepfather.

How did he appear?

Just as he did when he sexually abused her. He would approach her from the right through the door to her bedroom. That is, the inscape of her visual and auditory hallucinations was in the same configuration as that of the traumatic event. Moreover, she said that as a girl, whenever she felt her anger with stepfather's sexual abuse, she felt like killing herself.

Her psychotic experience was in the nature of a flashback; it was a reconstruction—intrusive, specific, and overwhelming—and it contained the awful and unique circumstances of an event she was unable to work through on her own. The intolerable truth clotted into the structure of her hallucinations.

Our literature is filled with accounts of the specificity of trauma living on with remarkable vitality, precise sensations triggering flashback phenomena. While playing basketball, one patient tells me, he ran off the court into some weeds, and was instantly back into the jungles of Viet Nam, hyperalert and shaking.

Case Example: White Noise

In this case example, a trauma creates its own *internal* sensation, a hallucination that must be expunged. Curiously, the outside voice had invaded this woman's insides: the internal had become external in space, but within her own body.

An old woman, thin and sad and with long flowing hair sits next to me. Her ear lobes are painted white. The medical student said she had used typewriter white-out fluid. Her teeth, too, are painted.

Why erasing fluid on the ears? While we were driving together in the car my oldest daughter once jokingly told me to turn up the music, that it was too quiet and she could hear herself think. White noise. Hearing too much, thinking too much. I surmised that there was something she could not bear to hear, and I told this old woman my thought. Sadly, she replied that her son had died, that he had killed himself shortly before she had come to the hospital. She had been told all of this by her nursing home caretakers. I thought I understood: She couldn't bear this news.

No, she explained, it wasn't the awful news so much — it was hearing his voice inside her head that she couldn't stand. The white-out was to get rid of his voice, to blank it out.

I asked about her son. He had been a good boy, who worked hard at a job that was beneath him. He had loved his wife and daughter and his wife left him for another man. He had never gotten over this grief, particularly not being able to see his daughter. Faithfully he had come to see his mother; she had never known about his self-torture, he had protected her. He had always been this way. She looked back in regret over her lifetime as a mother: She had become sick when he was just a boy; she too had been in love with a spouse who had treated her wrongly. Her poor boy had been on his own then too. He had been very handsome and independent. Perhaps his suicide had been a result of her inadequacies as a mother. This story was sketched simply, with few words.

Why the teeth covered with white-out? She had tried to swallow the white-out to remove him from inside of her. She looked up at me with tears in her eyes, "I guess the voices have to do with my not being ready to give him up yet" — and she cried. I had not expected this degree of insight; she no longer seemed psychotic. She was an old woman grieving her son, filled with regrets and guilt about her mothering, and she was just now beginning to give up her boy.

This woman had attempted to obliterate her internal experience. The observer witnesses the terrible internal struggle — there was more there than meets the eye. Sometimes though the stage is deceiving, there is less there than projected by the irritable eye of the observer. It is as if the empathizer is invited to have the affect and fantasy that eludes the person herself.

Case Example: A Gut-Wrenching Puzzle in an Empty Inscape

We are empathizers by nature, and we imaginatively project ourselves on to others in the commerce of everyday life. And so it is easy to be deceived by the apparent concordance of familiar symbols of affective life. We complete the picture of the other on limited information; we assume a fullness of experience.[3] It can be discordant and unsettling when, as in this case, these illusions break down.

This is a dream of a man in his early thirties and has recurred for several years prior to his starting therapy:

> Someone is throwing a pebble into a pile and tells me to find it. The implication is that if I do I will win the princess. But I have no idea what to do, or how to go about it, or even what to look for. It all has this nightmarish quality.

The dream telling itself has the quality of a frustrating but important puzzle, like the riddle of the sphinx. I try to establish for myself the inscape—and find myself perplexed and frustrated too. "Who," I ask, "is throwing the pebble?"

"I don't know who it is." Later, "Perhaps a man."

"The princess in the dream seems important. Could you tell me about her?"

"It is only a turn of phrase; there is no real princess in the dream. It means somehow that my life will be OK."

"How about the pebbles?" I ask.

"This part changes from dream to dream. The dream is always the same except that the pebble might be a piece of corn or any small, indistinguishable thing, like sand." There are no tactile or visual elements to mark them.

For each dimension I try to define with my patient we come up with no vivid sensory detail. Regarding time: The dream "never ends—but I just seem to wake up in the middle of the dream, until the next time." The space of the dream is indeterminate; it is not clearly day or night. Indeed, there are no strong experiential elements except for a vague sense of anxiety and unpleasantness. Listening, I feel queasy, restless, and unable to quite imagine the dream. It is a hopeless conceptual task, a mind-boggling riddle for a theoretical princess, all drained of color and life.

During this session he reflects on his life. He feels badly that he cares about no-one and that no-one cares about him: "I was always an outsider." He muses that though he is bright and with an advanced education, he works in a low-paying, pressured and meaningless bureaucratic job. But, he remarks, he really aspires to nothing else; perhaps some time he will prepare a résumé. Growing up in his family he felt apart, the distant one. Now if his parents should die he would not know what to feel; in fact, it would be a relief — he would not have to deal with them anymore. In the past year his mother had been near to death and he had felt empty and confused, vaguely thinking that it should all matter — but it never did. He reminds me of Camus's *Stranger*: "What difference could it make to me, the deaths of others, or a mother's love . . . ?"

He ruminates on the one relationship in his life that he misses. She was beautiful; he liked being seen with her (perhaps, I think, she is the princess), but for him there was no depth or real caring and after several years she dropped him, just like that. As in the dream there have been "no beginnings or endings to my relationships — they just sort of stop. 'Not with a bang, but a whimper.'" Like an infinite stretch of sand or an indistinguishable pile of corn, his life has had a vacant homogeneity, the people are faceless.

Somehow, he says, he just "never got it," nothing seemed to matter and time just slipped by: "Things just rolled in and out of my life — there are no milestones." For him time is indeed like sand; it has no markers, no sense of organization, no distinguishing features. Past, present, future have lost their meaning and he is trapped in the unending present. Life no longer flows: it has become a stagnant pool (Minkowski, 1970; Binswanger, 1975). The past seems unfilled, devoid of strong memories; unable to project into the future, he feels despair and a loss of hope. Perhaps, he thinks, he will kill himself in the next 10 years. In his dream, as in his life, he is like the prisoner in Kafka's *Trial*: He feels a muddy panic that his life is slipping away, that he heads toward his death not even knowing how to ask the question that would help him save himself. His existence is a nightmarish puzzle with no outline, no form, no beginning, no end — and not even a prayer.

Previously, I had often found it difficult to empathize with this man. His sessions were a litany of grievances. His body seemed detached and a bother. His bowels were merciless to him, painful and unpredictable and interfering with his life. While exploring this dream with him, I became aware of a nagging background feeling in my own body — my guts vaguely hurt. I now better understood his life's stance and dilemma. Ironically, it is the very absence of vibrant perceptual elements that gives his dream, his experience of life, such a distinctive and despairing quality.

Only much later did it occur to me that this barren inscape was one face of the clinical description of "alexithymia" (Sifneos, 1972, and Nemiah, 1984) with its paucity of fantasy, limited direct experience of affect, and predilection to psychosomatic expression. This compounded things; the dream predicts and reflects a general impasse in the therapy itself, that my focus on feeling and fantasy was inherently baffling to him. Even given the fact that this dream had been recurrent *prior* to therapy, it was no doubt now a transference dream too, reaching down into earlier experiences of frustrating and uncomprehending others and feeding on itself in the interpersonal circularity of his affective dullness and confusion. Transference is simply a translation of previous experience onto a present one—how could it be otherwise? The very setting of our relationship with its subtle demands and implicit promises must have felt an impossible task: I was now that someone, also indistinguishable, throwing a pebble into a pile and telling him to find it.

If feeling, fantasy, and sensation were constricted, is it no wonder that this man would focus on his physical pain? What could be realer? It is a common story among self destructive patients that the cigarette burns to the skin, the repetitive knife strokes to the arm, are mercifully clarifying at a time of inner chaos and storm. A focus or calmness descends, a release. Apart from the masochistic implications for unconscious guilt and the recreation of early objects, there is another restitutive function: the pain itself is centering, the fragments of self cohere around the intensity—I hurt, therefore I am.[4] Sensation and affect coalesce within the architecture of the self.

Case Example: Reality, Olfaction, and the Vast Structure of Recollection

We take sensation for granted as our medium—until it fails us. With the diminution of sensory organs, the margins of reality blur. Deaf people or even those amidst an alien language are prone to paranoia. Night staff on medical wards come to anticipate "sundowning," the diurnal delirium of the sensory deprived, those wrenched from familiar environments and struggling to maintain a connection to the outside world (and this is why turning on lights and a radio helps). What is subtler to appreciate is the role of perception in maintaining the coherence of our *inner* world, that through sensation we link ourselves not only to the outside present but to the inner structure of life's experience.

In the midst of these considerations I learned of a man who had a sudden and dense loss of his sense of smell.[5] With nostalgia and bitterness he described the loss of intensity of commonplace experience. He mourned the spontaneous richness of the ordinary enlivened by the taste and smell of previous recollection. That is, in losing his sense of smell he had also lost a critical evocative and *associative* function of memory.

The luxuriousness of an afternoon in May, for example, comes alive not only in the smell of a spring shower, but also in a distinctive personal olfactory presence with its rush of memory of other rains and other times.

Such experiences will die in a memory deprived of nutrient sensations from the present. Olfaction was an intimate part of this man's experience of his life and himself, an associative glue integrating his world, past and present. An internal organizer of memory, and consequently *present* experience, had disappeared. Through body and sensation memory stimulates perceived present, and present influences recollected past.

The above are examples of specific sensory details that presented themselves in the course of clinical work. One learns the ways people organize experience and create a coherent sense of themselves through their sensory world view. The relationship between inscape and self is reciprocal, complex, and paradoxical. In later chapters I will shift the emphasis to that circularity itself. At this stage in my pursuit of *Einfühlung* I became more aware of the frozen potential of much of described experience—that a fuller understanding lay dormant in the crystallized possibilities of images, sensations, and inchoate emblems of the other's distinctive world view. Active empathy, as opposed to the notion of a more passive and resonant empathy, could literally open doors.

CHAPTER 4

Active Empathy:
The Dormant Inscape

*The past is hidden somewhere outside the realm, beyond the reach of intellect, in some material object (in the sensation which the material object will give us) which we do not suspect.
. . . the smell and taste of things remain poised a long time, like souls, ready to remind us, waiting and hoping for their moment
. . . and bear unfaltering, in the tiny and almost impalpable drop of their essence, the vast structure of recollection.*

—MARCEL PROUST

I n phenomenology there is a concept, "inner horizon," to describe the fullness of sensory experience given the perceiver's narrow perspective (Husserl, 1962; Ihde, 1977). Though we see an object in only a limited view, we nevertheless implicitly experience it as deeper and fuller. A book, for example, may present itself to me as a two-dimensional blue profile, yet I know that it has other aspects that I cannot see but that feel there to me. To quote Ihde (1977, p. 63), "I do not see the world without 'thickness' nor do I see it as a mere façade. What appears does so as a play of presence and a specific absence-within-presence." Through Picasso's eyes we see something as if all at once and from multiple perspectives simultaneously.

To describe this, phenomenologists use words similar to psychoanalytic dream language, for example, "manifest" and "latent." By contrast though, the psychoanalytic sense of latent refers to meaning hidden from awareness by a dynamic unconscious. I am stressing here a different sense of latent, that of the fullness of an object as constituted by the perceiver.

I would like to extend this notion of latent even further—to one that is simultaneously perceptual, symbolic, and unconscious. There is a fullness of experience that is embodied in its *potential*. A door in a dream implies another side of the door and another space. It invites, even demands, an opening—or a firmly keeping shut—as part of its very being as a door. A dream door bears not only associated past significance but also possibilities; that is, it is a nexus of latent and diverging futures. Picasso-like we could look at front, back, inside, outside, past, present, future, and all at once. The phenomenologically latent is also highly significant for the latent unconscious meaning; the two are linked.

Case Example: On Being Torn Up Inside

A woman has the following dream: "Gorillas are tearing up a house, breaking the windows."

She has no initial associations to the dream, except that it seems odd and upsetting. I ask her what the house was like, and she observes that it was an old, two story white farm house with three windows on the bottom and a sagging porch. The windows were broken out.

Her dream experience is of looking at the house from the outside. The insides, though, are very much implied. Windows, looking in, looking out, broken out, broken in, inside, outside—and so I ask, "What was the inside of the house like?" Perhaps we might explore the interior of the house, open the dream door and walk in.

"Funny," she muses, "I never actually saw the inside of the house in the dream, but I did imagine it somehow." Though she has great difficulty describing the experience, she knew this implicitly and without actually experiencing the inside as an image. That is, it was an absence-in-presence, an almost-conscious fantasy within a dream. It reminds her, she says, of another powerful image, a Tarzan movie in which apes had torn apart a house, destroying it, making a terrible mess on the inside, throwing stuff everywhere.

She is a single woman, in her forties, recently disappointed in love, and she is still grieving. She had just undergone an emergency gynecological procedure and had this dream the first night of her return home from the hospital—alone. Her fears are of aging, never getting married or having children. With familiar surprise I note to myself that neither the context of the dream nor her concerns about her body were close to consciousness in the telling of the dream. Nevertheless, my own sense of her fears seemed more empathically vivid to me: She must have felt torn up inside, violated, and left a mess. The house seemed old to her and with a sagging porch—and I ask her about this specific bodily concern. She remarks with embarrassment that after the procedure she had the fear that her uterus would "turn inside out," that there would no longer be any internal support for it, that it might drop through her vagina. She had worried that she would lose her womb altogether, that her insides would fall out.

There were other levels of meaning. She had come to treatment after terminating a psychotherapy in which the therapist had made advances to her. Initially she had been flattered but then felt bewildered and furious— she had fallen in love with him and now was in a rage by this breach of ethics and lack of interest for her well-being. Emotionally she had felt torn apart inside. This had been of great concern in starting a new therapeutic relationship and was intensely felt throughout the initial phases of her therapy with me (and was one hazard of taking a potentially intrusive psychotherapeutic approach, for example, opening dream doors). The issue of betrayal and lack of concern by others, moreover, had deep resonant roots with earlier life experiences.

On the night of her return home from surgery the dream of a broken and neglected house symbolically captured her concern about her body. The visual presentation in the dream was of a falling apart outside; latent in the image—the absence-in-presence—was the broken and torn apart insides; and latent within all of this were both adult and childhood hurts still alive and pressing for expression and resolution in her outside life and in the transference, that is, the latent unconscious. Like Russian dolls, possibilities were nested within possibilities.

Words like "symbol," by definition "something that stands for or represents another thing" (*Webster's Unabridged Dictionary*, 2nd Ed.), become inadequate for our meaning in these situations. For us as listeners a symbol seems derivative, to mean something else. We infuse meaning and energy into our observer's experience by making the symbol come alive through its complex, overdetermined and ambiguous status, like a pun. For the dreamer the symbol is *lived in itself* and does not feel secondary or a point-to-point correspondence to another thing. By interpreting it as a symbol, I the listener *create* it as a symbol. Before my action on it, the budding symbol existed as part of the inscape of the other—and achieved its power through its mysterious and pregnant (!) status.

Freud (1900) observed this with so-called "universal" symbols, noting that there was something about a powerful symbol that made it difficult for people to elaborate further in associative fashion. Such symbols are virtual bedrock. My patient, too, did not readily get what seemed obvious to me on listening to her dream—that the house "meant" her body. I thought about and to some extent empathized with her experiencing the house image; she, however, *lived* it. The dictionary meaning of latent, "lying hidden and undeveloped within a person or thing, as a quality or power" (*Webster's Unabridged*, 2nd Ed.), captures the vitality of the dynamic symbols that we live through: They have a nascent power, undeveloped and waiting. We do not reveal symbols so much as we release them.

Frozen Time

> And these moments of the past do not remain
> still; they retain in our memory the motion
> which drew them towards the future—towards
> a future which has itself become the past—
> drawing us along in their train.
>
> —MARCEL PROUST

> Every dream is a potential nightmare.
>
> —ANGEL GARMA

Lived experience streams within the kinetics of a future about to unfold. One can never recapture the experience of reading a particular novel for the first time—the unknown possibilities of the initial reading have been foreclosed the second time around, both limiting and, occasionally, deepening our subsequent experience. Similarly, recalled and narrated experience, as opposed to the actual lived moment, seldom retains the freshness of possibilities, the open-endedness of the future.

And our possible futures themselves are always in flux. The quality of our expectations, fears and hopes change as we change. We recall our past futures with nostalgia, sadness or relief: This is who I was then, awaiting this or that event, fearing, hoping, anticipating. That is, we have *remembered* futures, a future, say, that a child once hoped for and that is now impossible, a future that no longer exists. These recollected futures are comparable to the antique futures of old science fiction movies or to the peculiarly constricted visions of the already run-down 1967 World's Fair in Montreal or the Tomorrowland of Disney World. These are now dated futures that could only belong to a particular social time and space. By putting the wish as the impetus of the dream, Freud implicitly embedded it in a dynamic matrix of events: The dream, though drawing its life from the past, pushed toward the wish of a new future. This of course is paradigmatic for human existence in general. Time itself presents a complex matrix of absence-within-presence, a vector and context for the obscure potential of desire, hope, and fear.

Is there a way of getting to the possibilities of the lived world of the other, the truncated futures not always immediately available in the telling, perhaps eclipsed by defenses as well as by our failure to consider? I am reminded of interactive novels, movies, or even computer games that provide branch points for the participant to change the narrative direction: Though we recall events fixed in time, the lived moments themselves are always on the cusp of possibilities. In empathizing with Hamlet we defy logic, we wonder if it could be otherwise than the way we know it must, has, and will always turn out. To enter into Hamlet's drama empathically we have to suspend our knowledge that the narrative is inevitable: For Hamlet it is the agony of choice, of alternatives.[1]

In the following vignette, I had the chance to open such a dialogue with the inherent possibilities of a patient's waking fantasies. The images that came to his mind had the odd quality of frozen motion, like a still photograph of a boat approaching a waterfall. One could not imagine the image (that is, empathize) without considering the potential consequences. The *suspense* of the fantasy lay beyond its mere *suspension* of action: The suspense itself meant unbearable possibilities. Freezing time was a freezing of awareness, a magical staving off of the imminent next frame.

CASE EXAMPLE: A DESPERATE MOMENT

A young man rising in his profession had recently turned down the opportunity to apply for a position of prominence for which he felt qualified, one that his superiors had encouraged him to consider. Though many aspects of the job were appealing to him, he disliked himself when he had power and authority, feeling that he became too grandiose and manipulative of others. In the midst of these struggles he experienced several spontaneous and vivid fantasy images, daydream in quality.

The first of these occurred to him in a group setting of his peers and a senior corporate manager. He imagined that all of his peers were gone from the meeting and that he was left alone with this boss — and that there would be a fight to the death. I asked about his image, what he experienced. It was, he explained, the picture of his boss lying on his back with blood over his heart. He had a closely allied image of his own drowning in a pool of water in the board room — and no one helping. He then visualized his father watching him drown.

I ask him what he experiences in the fantasy image. "My father is standing there."

And is there more? "No one is helping."

Perhaps there's an image of your father? "Well he's laughing. That's about it." Despite the vivid scene, all of this is related with a detached, bland affect. He seems stuck.

I say, "Let's try an experiment of sorts. Imagine what you would say to your father if you were in that particular situation."

With unexpected and intense feeling he blurts out, "I'm sorry! I'm sorry I always beat you out. I'm sorry that Mom loved me more, that I was better than you."

And father? "He says, 'You deserve it!' And he is very sadistic and laughing: He wants me to be in pain, to suffer."

Associations now tumble out. He recalls being a very young child at the beach. Somehow he got caught in a "whirlpool—it must have been an undertow"—and he grew panicky. No matter how hard he tries he cannot get back to shore. He screams and cries. He recalls his brother looking at him paralyzed. His grandmother is on the shore also panicked—but unable to help. Suddenly, a man appears, as if out of nowhere, and plucks him out. He can't remember his face.

He recalls having loved his father at one time, but that his father was inept and bumbling. He had once been proud of his father for performing magic tricks for his fifth grade class, but had then been fearful about his father dying of a heart attack.

Later I ask whether any of these images seem to relate to me. He thinks of the man who plucked him from the water.

With the tired-good feeling that often accompanies a session of intense feeling, he relates that he has never understood why he has so hated authority and, gritting his teeth, "why I'll do anything to thwart an authority figure, anything, even if it hurts me." This is merely a beginning. In future sessions he was to explore his deeper feelings about me and how he has often wanted me to fail to help him—because for me to help would mean that I would then beat him by being successful in my work.

In this therapeutic moment the affect and dialogue were locked within the spliced out segment of the fantasy—the implications were left dormant. Note that I am not trying to create a new outcome here, a new internal dialogue per se with the internalized object (for example, "Now imagine your father responding differently").[2] Such a dialogue may, of course, suggest itself or elucidate reasons why it was never possible. My goal, though, is a clarification of the experience, an extension of my empathic understanding. If the therapy is successful these internal dialogues will spontaneously change.

Empathic Travels

> *So say whatever goes through your mind. Act as though, for instance, you were a traveller sitting next to the window of a railway carriage and describing to someone inside the carriage the changing views which you see outside.*
>
> —FREUD (1913, p. 135)

As I become engaged with the inner life of another, I experience a growing sense of familiarity with a built-up internal landscape. Oftentimes this is not so conscious to me. I enter a private world constructed from associations and images stimulated by my patient and drawn from my own personal past experience. But it is a new world to me and one that usually remains quite separate from the worlds I have entered in my experiences with other people. I often wonder—and patients will sometimes ask—how I keep the stories, the histories, separate after having heard so many. But I usually do; each is so different to me that it is remarkably effortless. My experience of listening to case conferences or supervision is much different. I simply do not hold on to the details over time with the same ease: It is work. It is the here-and-now experience of the person and our relationship (including the intense transference and countertransference affects), along with the parallel unique inscape that develops in my mind's eye, that keeps the different clinical experiences so separate.

Often I am surprised by a new detail of the inscape—it does not fit with the internal world that I have constructed of the other. These discrepancies are invariably interesting. For example, why do I presently notice this inconsistency and does it point to my own filter on things? Or is this new facet only now able to come alive and into view; that is, previously the picture had been boldly, perhaps defensively, painted without this new nuance of love or hatred? Does it represent a shift in our relationship, that I am now privy to aspects of self that seemed too unsafe to present to me before? Has a resistance been lifted with a freeing up of the other's inner life? Are new inner structures coming into being, supporting new potentials for world view? There is an abundance of possibilities. It is as if I am reworking a very large three dimensional map (including time, four dimensions) painted with sadness, love, hatred, memories, possibilities—one that I have been constructing silently, effortlessly, in my involvement with the other. The map can only be a map, an imagined correspondence that barely reflects the true internal experience of the other. It is a map constructed second-hand from another's life's travels, a map that undergoes constant reworking, revision (re-vision), and clarification.

It may seem odd to describe clinical work in this fashion, clearly other metaphors might be used. In fact, I suspect these projected empathic landscapes are a common experience of everyday life. Certainly, it is one of the surprises and disappointments of seeing favorite plays or novels put into film or theater—the actors are not what we had come to imagine, even though what we *had* imagined may never have been articulated so clearly before. But it certainly was not *this* actor who is too tall, sinister, angular, swarthy. . . . In such moments I become aware of some expectations that I bring with me. For my children, I suspect, the real Alice in Wonderland will always live in the Disney inscape; any other rendition would seem fraudulent, not right.

Interestingly, a significant part of therapeutic work may be in just this linking and revision of the conflicting or unarticulated aspects of the inscape. Frequently my confusion about events and details may reflect the other's inner clouding or fragmentation of experience. It is in our mutual attempt to help *me* understand, for the patient to feel understood, that these experiences are rewoven into a coherent narrative and concomitant psychic fabric.

In Proust's search for the past he found that access to memory resides in the sensation of the object, awaiting our re-experience. These Proustian sensations, however, are like switch points or crossroads—they are often the nexus of many memories that intersect and fan out from that singular and organizing sensory center of our recollection. And so it is here, at these affectively charged nodal points, that memories, complexes, can be claimed again as part of a larger whole.[3]

As I gain greater familiarity with the world of the other, I then have a Proustian echo of recollection. With one patient, for example, I recall a farm in my mind's eye, the fields, the roads, the old lady who fed the patient/me ginger snaps and bananas—all experiences I have lived empathically through her. I do not recall in my own life whether I have ever even had ginger snaps and bananas together, but I can almost taste them on my mind's tongue. Moreover, I sometimes recollect such empathic sensations more readily than does the patient from whom I have learned them! In different contexts the patient may put these too painful sensations out of consciousness; for the therapist the sensations do not have the same intensity (nor, to be sure, does the therapist have the same defensive structure, no matter how empathic). This, I think, is the basis of many therapeutic hunches and intuitions that seem out of the blue. It is not merely my reaching into resonant experience from my own life (for example, that I have, parallel to the patient, fond boyhood memories of eating cookies and feeling happy and secure). It is more: *I now have memories empathically derived and elaborated into a relatively coherent form from someone else's experience.* I have incorporated the other's experience into my own paler version; I reach deep down into my internalized inscape of the other.

CASE EXAMPLE: A NIGHTMARE'S LANDSCAPE

A woman awakens terrified from the following dream:

> My son and I were going to a park, just for a walk. We were separated — no, he ran up ahead and I started to go up into a town, a small rural town, and I started to go up the road between two buildings. There was a feedmill and a bridge or a walkway connecting two buildings and there were men hanging from the walkway and grabbing people as they walked that way. And my son was ahead of me and I went another way and I got to the park. And there was this row of doors, and I kept opening the door to see if my son were there and he wasn't — and I was absolutely terrified and then I woke up. And I kept thinking something had happened to him and he wasn't there. And I thought I wasn't there and if he cried out I wouldn't be there.
>
> The other part of the dream that stands out is the road that was around the feed mill — it was full of ruts and like covered with shit and very slippery and difficult to walk on. And I remember looking down at it and I was surprised and I just kept walking. I was thinking that it was like the logging road to my son's camp which was covered with mud, and the rains made the ground so muddy.

She then associates to an unpleasant, extended argument with her husband while they had been driving to visit her son at camp, and how despairing, angry, and confused she had been. Her life has been filled with anxiety recently: She worries about her career, the family finances, her marriage, and her increasing preoccupation with me. She associates to some pleasant times with her husband, some nice moments in the bleakness — which only adds to her confusion about her life. Looking for peace of mind she often withdraws into herself, "It all seems pretty shitty to me — to get back to the image of the dream."

"The image captures it," I comment.

"(Sigh!) It certainly does."

I ask if she could describe her experience of that image further.

"It was surprising to me. It was sort of . . . the thing was, it was slippery and full of ruts. And I didn't want to fall down. It was like I thought I wouldn't get out — but I did. I remember there being a building and the road coming down out of the building and down the hill and when I was on the hill, that's when I realized what it was. It was full of ruts, and not soft, but hard and I was sinking into it and I was sliding over it, afraid I'd fall. . . . There wasn't a smell. It was sort of like coming upon it and being surprised and when I realized what it was, but rather than being caught up, I had to get where I was going, I had to get to the park. Being more scared kept me from being bogged down."

Throughout this narrative I had been forming another impression that was like a déjà vu to me. I had experienced it before, though it felt strange and uncanny to me, a compound sensory image that she had once described with vivid and distressing affect. The mental representation I had was strong with a slippery feeling, a tactile and kinesthetic sensation that was not part of her original description of the event or even how I recalled it as told by her, but that now seemed integral. I hesitated to comment, wondering if this image were my projection onto her dream. So many things to explore, too many things that one could pursue with such a dream (for example, her concern about her son seemed vivid and pressing; certainly her own fears of abandonment by me and by others were common concerns in her treatment; she had often expressed apprehension of being bogged down in the psychotherapy, of being fearful of what might be dredged up). Awkwardly I decided to go with my hunch, "I am not sure of its relevance, but it reminds me of the scene you once described of being a little girl and watching the pigs being slaughtered—I don't know if it's the slippery part of the image that seems a part of it, though you hadn't described it that way."

"It's funny," she reflected, "That was sort of blood and guts, and slippery. There was a barn there—a *red* barn. Its like when you hang a pig up after you slaughter it; it's like those men hanging in the dream . . . just suspended there."

And so I realized the landscapes *were* linked: the red barn and hanging bodies—I had not consciously thought of them, but now I could see and feel the inscape, the blood and shit-slippery surface, and now the men—"Like slaughtered pigs?" I say.

"Yeah, the way they were suspended. The feed mill in the dream was old and painted red too. *Last night* I went outside into the garden to plant holly hocks . . . they were blossoming. My neighbor grew them."

I think, holly hocks, ham hocks. "The neighbor who had the pig slaughter?"

"Yes!" she laughs, "I also remember once sliding down her walkway during a light snow and I ran right into her husband and knocked him down." He was the one who slaughtered the pigs.

This particular session ended, with many loose threads, some picked up in future sessions. The nightmare's horrific quality involved threat of great harm to her son. And it drew power from her own childhood imprint, a landscape of squealing, then eviscerated, pigs dripping blood and shit as a young girl watched in fascinated horror.

In retrospect there seem many similarities between the two scenes, one dreamt and one remembered: Hanging bodies, red barns, slippery ground, fright. In linking these landscapes in my own mind—through my *imagination* of her dream and my *imagination* of her memory—I established a resonant connection that extended into this woman's childhood memories, compartmentalized and split-off memories filled with violence both witnessed and imagined. Other connections were established: her fascination with violent men, her father's hunting which seemed so grotesque and frightening to her as a little girl, and the fact that when she entered into treatment she was exposing herself to some very real potential violence in her everyday life.

What does it mean that the total sensory experience of traumatic events are burned into the memory with such an intrusive power? It is not just the overpowering affect—but the sensations themselves that give the recollected experiences such a here-and-now existence, suspended but ready to spring to life: "the smell and taste of things remain poised a long time, like souls, ready to remind us, waiting and hoping for their moment" (Proust). These events are lived as if in a present scene, a "flashback": In a flash one is back in the event, smelling it, tasting it, seeing it, living it. Apart from massive trauma it seems as if the trauma of everyday life, too, resides in the senses.

I do not know where in my own background such a sensory imaginative response of sliding on blood would come from. After this event occurred I read of a Viet Nam veteran's post-traumatic recall of being caught in a mortar attack: "There was blood everywhere . . . on the bodies, the body bags, and the helicopter floor. Everything was slippery from the blood on it. Since then, the smell of blood makes me want to cry. It makes me want to get a fan to get the smell out of me" (Kline, 1985). I *imagined* a latent sensation that linked aspects of the inscape of another's internal life—but how is it that such a dormant and hitherto unexpressed impression come to me as listener? On the edge of my awareness I had constructed a riveting traumatic inscape in parallel detail to her experience. In a manner of speaking, I had slipped on the ground of her inscape!

In an edge-of-consciousness way I entered my patient's separate experiences, which then remained *in my mind* with their own intense sensory traces, ready to come to life.[4] Despite the ultimate unknowability of the other, there was a coherence of world view that I could approximate from within my own distinctive world view. Moreover, this coherence extended into the shadows of her inscape, into its dormant possibilities. That is to say, *the inscape of this other person had its heretofore unelaborated absence-in-presence that became articulated in my own mental representation of her experience.* It was through the empathic dialectic that I then brought into consciousness my experience of her inscape, which was then affirmed in her connecting to my connections, pushing the spiral of understanding further. We explored reflected inscapes together, me blind and imagining, her frightened and recoiling.

The relationship of the empathizer to the other is, of course, paradoxical. Because empathy is by definition the "imaginative projection of one's own consciousness into another being," we will unavoidably find ourselves reflected within our gaze toward the other. I look for you and see myself; I have no choice but to draw on what I know and feel. But because I can reflect on this enigma itself, I have the possibility of expanding my personal experience beyond its margins. In looking for you, I must identify my own reflection and continually put myself aside. And so empathy inheres in the subtle surprise of the other, those aspects both familiar enough to draw on my own experience and yet unique and unfamiliar enough to force me to accommodate my imaginative projection.[5]

PART III
An Extended Search

All the residuum of reality . . . which cannot be transmitted in talk . . . that ineffable something which differentiates qualitatively what each of us has felt and what he is obliged to leave behind at the threshold of the phrases in which he can communicate . . .

—MARCEL PROUST

CHAPTER 5

An Extended Search:
Fragments of a Case

> *On things for which no*
> *wording can be found . . .*
> —JOHN KEATS

I n previous chapters I developed vignettes illustrative of specific points, and, as such, they are but pieces of clinical experiences. In this chapter I will, through an extended case example, explore a particular empathic dialogue over time, how my evolving appreciation of another's inner world changed and deepened, and indeed how I became woven into the very inscape that I was exploring. This will take us to further considerations of the nature of subjective inscapes and their dormant potentials, the experience of radical disjunctions of world view, the creation of meaning through metaphor and image, and how metaphors themselves come alive within a changing internal landscape. The chapter to follow this one, "Reflections on World View," will expand these themes and will serve as a broader theoretical explication.

Spaces Outside of Time

In the process of reviewing what I have written, I am often vexed by changes in tense and how blithely I mix past and present. Initially I would simply rework the text for narrative consistency. Finally it occurred to me that my inconsistency itself was worthy of investigation.[1]

To narrate a clinical vignette, I must at least temporarily have my reader in mind. This is a matter of empathy and a circular one at that. I am imagining the reader's experience in trying to comprehend my own. My task then is to help the reader empathize with my experience of trying to empathize with another. Can I anticipate points of confusion for all of these world views trying to assimilate one another? Ironically, it is in that reflection itself, in my trying to create a coherent narrative for the reader, that I then retrospectively clean up the experience and move away from it.[2]

The unedited version, tenses mixed, is closer to my empathic reality. As I recall my experience of my patient's experience, I often have a narrative frame around it, for example, "Several years ago I saw a man who . . . " I set the stage for my memory; it is in the past and I am recalling it from the distant present. But, as I get into the recalled experience itself and forget the reader, the past tense drops away and the present exerts itself—I am reliving the memory, but in a new space, in the present, but also outside of time. It has its own inscape.

Proust, empathizing with himself and his different selves past and present, observed:

> I compared these various happy impressions with one another and found that they had this in common, namely, that I felt them as though they were occurring simultaneously in the present moment and in some distant past, which the sound of the spoon against the plate, or the unevenness of the flagstones, or the peculiar flavor of the *madeleine* even went so far as to make coincide with the present, leaving me uncertain in which period I was. In truth, the person within me who was at this moment enjoying this impression enjoyed in it the qualities which it possessed that were common to both an earlier day and the present moment; and this person came into play only when, by this process of identifying past with present, he could find himself in the only environment in which he could live, that is to say, entirely outside of time.[3]

I had not initially planned on this chapter; it demanded, though, to be born. Its gestation was as follows. As I developed my thinking, I would draw examples from my clinical work, taking vignettes from my present experience and writing down what occurred while it was still fresh in my mind. More distantly recalled clinical experience had the disadvantage of my lapses of memory and my unconsciously and selectively recalling what had happened (which is interesting in its own right, but without the kind of experimental control that would be really edifying).

Over time I realized that several examples were drawn from the same person, someone whose treatment had begun and deepened during my writing. It seemed truer to put these vignettes together in one section than to scatter them throughout the text. Having made this decision late in the process, I wanted to avoid the temptation of a retrospective tidying up of the material to make it fit. Rather, it was not unlike stringing beads—I took what was already completed and provided the narrative thread.

And so the following material has rough edges, the advantage and disadvantage of being written in pieces at the time it actually occurred. This confers an air of immediacy and also of fragmentation—I was not writing with the more detached wisdom of several years post-treatment reflection. Despite Freud's admonition to avoid "speculation or brooding over cases while they are in analysis" and to submit "the material to a synthetic process of thought only after the analysis is concluded" (1912, p. 114), I wanted to capture an aspect of the empathic process that occurs in the here-and-now, that is incompletely formed and groping. My various understandings will, of course, continue to change over time. This material unfolded to me, as I hope it will unfold to the reader, and remains mysterious and incomplete, as indeed the experience of actually doing clinical work must always be.

The Texture of a Life: Beginning Treatment

She first felt she met me through the fabrics of my waiting room. This was unselfconscious for her, a way of taking in and experiencing the world. When younger she had wanted to be a weaver and, though that was old history, she had an awareness of and sensitivity to textures and materials that she took for granted.

For her my waiting room fabrics were warm and inviting. This apparent externality was critical and auspicious: Her previous therapist's office seemed confining and cold, unable to transcend its basement origins. She began that treatment out of a quiet desperation: Life had become dull, confusing, and passionless, with pervasive feelings of "loss, emptiness, aloneness and despair." The therapy had never taken hold. And though she did not like this woman therapist, she nevertheless felt a grudging respect for her honesty, directness, and willingness to refer her to someone else for a psychoanalysis. She spontaneously spoke about other important people in terms of their spatial impact on her, how they invaded her "boundaries."

Mother, I learned, had physically changed as my patient grew up. After the birth of another child, mother grew depressed and fatter at the same time. My patient had felt mother's corporeality as oppressive and smothering, overwhelming the tiny amount of family space. Outdoors and into the woods the little girl would escape from her mother—open space was freedom. She developed asthma in her teenage years, with several serious emergencies. As a woman she remained vigilant to the possibilities of entrapment and suffocation.

Here I am reminded of a child's story (*The Runaway Bunny*, by Margaret Brown) in which a loving mother becomes part of the larger scenery, incorporated as the wind, a mountain, a tree. I became associated with the warmth of texture, as the transference experience was taken up into my patient's sensory world view. Early on in the treatment she had a dream of entering a house, holding in her hand a piece of cloth. When I asked her what the experience of the cloth was like, she associated to my waiting room fabrics, that it had the same paisley pattern. The colors, though, were browner, like that of the Persian carpet hanging in my office. She had woven me into a symbolic fabric, a transitional object, knitting a connection to me and the various spaces that we shared. My couch had its own special feel, a ribbed woven material ("warm," "the little fibers" touched very lightly "feel like down"), and she would instinctively put her hands underneath her legs to press the texture onto her skin. The couch itself felt soothing, and in association she thought of her son's worn-out and beloved blanket, her own stuffed dog so important to her when she was five or six, and her love for her childhood family dog, shaggy and so calming.

Other textures, too, were richly evocative. The wallpaper in my office, a woven grass-cloth, had a distinctive and reassuring feel, and occasionally I noticed her hand rub up against the wall as if exploring it. The chairs in my office were a surprise to her, covered with a "golden velour" (to me merely a dirty wide-ribbed corduroy in need of replacement), and they brought back to her memories of an old family sofa, a couch she had loved.

Pieces of clothes are of great importance to her. A favorite sweater, blue with a wide soft weave, felt unusually comfortable. It had a history, given to her by a woman who aroused passionate feelings—longing, hatred, and love. She would wear this sweater with some matching gloves, a gift from a close male friend. While wearing these clothes she was always aware, in the periphery of her mind, that these were gifts from special people whose presence remained with her.

Memories live in the textures around her, Proustian—"poised a long time, like souls, ready to remind." A teacher comes alive in the evocation of her colors, textures, and weaves: "My first grade teacher, a sweet old lady, pretty in a classy way . . . always wore these nice knit sweaters . . . rouge . . . with gray hair tinted blue . . . and short and wrinkled. . . . She had a fur coat that matched her lavender car. I used to love to feel her coat . . . a flat fur, like a seal. It was very sleek."

In one dream from this beginning period she had an image of an older woman who, dream fashion, was *my* mother, wearing "green, a very soft wool dress . . . she *felt* soft, her presence . . . soothing." Her own mother is also in the dream, with a peculiar and uneven, lurching presence—she just pops up and then is gone, jarring and unpleasant. In contrast to her mother, my mother is a calming presence. As she talks about the image of the wonderful soft green wool, her voice becomes peaceful. Later, the mere conjuring up of that image of the wool skirt on my mother produces the same marked change in affect, a serenity descends around her.

In a larger sense this theme of textures and touching is one of making contact, and it pervades her awareness of life. In our sessions the beginning of the hour is often difficult; she will seem uncertain and hesitant: "I'm always wondering where you are at. . . . I think in the process of the hour there develops some sort of connectedness that isn't there at the beginning." She must first locate me and my affective state so that she then can act accordingly. "I gear my response to what I expect others want." (Has this been the case around the material I am presenting? Is she responding to my particular interests? Would another therapist have heard this material differently, and would she have complied, creating a different language, a different way of connecting? How do I untangle her wish to please me and the fact that she listens to how I listen to her?)

My very words, too, can have the effect of calming her, orienting her, of transforming a negative affect into a positive one. The weave of my words has become palpable; it is her connection to me: "*Here*, when you respond or understand, it's *so amazing*." Kohut once remarked that feeling understood is the adult equivalent of being held.

These omnipresent and intertwined themes of touching and texture, space and distance, darkness and aloneness are, of course, all part of a larger concern with being mothered, fed, made contact with. She has met these needs largely through the men in her life. Not surprisingly, she associated this to her mother and the frustration in connecting to her; she had turned to her father for affection and involvement. And her search for a motherly man had at times taken on a compulsive and sexual quality.

The road, though, leads back to her mother. One is reminded of Harlow's work (1958) on the tactile aspects of mothering and self-soothing. I imagine her early futile search for an involved, comforting, and containing mother led to her own holding of herself through materials and other transitional phenomena, all coming alive in the very experience of her everyday world and of our beginning relationship. (And this is another facet of the technical word "reconstruction," that we recreate a world view in the present, assuming that it extends back into time over a life's trajectory.)

As with all beginning treatments and learning of someone's life, it is difficult to know at first what elements will remain as recurrent themes. I did not fully realize (that is, I only nearly knew) when I wrote these pages that texture and space would become so critical in her subsequent experience of me as our relationship unfolded. But this was to be expected: Space is the medium of connectedness and separation, and each sensory modality will have its own unique relationship to it. Later my tampering with my office structure and surroundings (that is, remodeling) would hold deep importance.

Red Rockets

I soon became aware of a resistance to the treatment relationship itself. I thought it must be in part a consequence of the fearful intensity this woman had experienced with key figures in her life. In the past she had felt "sexually addicted" to relationships and frightened by her out of control behavior. With her mother experienced as deadened and not able to give freely, she must have turned to her gregarious and lively father with an urgency she was to experience later in her adult heterosexual relationships. The maternal longings, expressed in her search for a caring man, were central features of the treatment, and they frightened her. She became alarmed by her increasing dependence on and preoccupation with me, struggling even to talk about it, avoiding it for fear of actualizing it. She fears overwhelming me, as she has others, with her intensity and need.

In a session soon after my having been away she says, lively and flirtatiously, "When you were away, I thought I'd like to give you a big hug to welcome you back," and thinks of shocking me with outrageous behavior. In a sense, she wants to get a rise out of me. "I'm *delighted* you're back." Competitive themes with my wife arose: Who decorated my office? She noticed "steamy" songs on the radio—and wished to share them with me. Her dreams had oral and sexualized overtones, for example, of being in my office, eating grapes and spitting out the seeds.

There was an urgent need for me to be steadily there: "Please don't go anyplace . . . remain constant." "Can I trust you to be here?" "Oh, what would I do without you?" Early memories emerged of mother's drinking and screaming. Mother made her throw away the empty bottles in a creek so father wouldn't know. "She'd make life miserable—I'd do it to keep the peace—swearing me to secrecy." She recalled her anger, loneliness and shame about mother—and how she had not wanted to acknowledge the pain of those years for fear that it was an integral part of her self, a kind of destructive legacy. If only mother had shown some interest. She had memories of her asthma as an adolescent, feeling stifled and smothered by mother.

During this time she developed an intense rivalry and hatred for a female boss whom she could neither respect nor bear to be controlled by; it was a clash interwoven with a life or death intensity. The work space itself felt oppressive, with her boss continually intruding, and this resonated with her feelings about her mother. An excerpt from a session during this time:

(She cries softly.) "It's funny I don't know why I'm crying. . . . It has to do with I'm here and you're here and it's safe."

"A life space."

"Yes. It's like I can breathe."

"Yes—and that's come up before: smothering, breathing—you also had asthma as a girl."

"(Laughs) I know. I know. I'm so aware of that. I'm not sure I understand, but it's sort of like your words allow me to breathe, and there's some sense of relief. . . . I don't ever feel trapped in here. Quite to the contrary. I feel like there's a lot of space."

Space is not metaphor for her—it is tangible, physical. Her yearnings for me to take care of her ran deeply (along with homosexual dreams and fantasies), in a maternal transference in the person of the motherly man. "I'm reminded of dream I had about you. I wouldn't talk about it before. I was having dinner—and you didn't have on a shirt. And what I thought about then—and now—is just wanting to curl up and put my head against your chest and just be held . . . the image is both soothing and painful at the same time." I ask her why it may have been threatening to say this to me, and she talks about her fear of being criticized. In subsequent sessions she broached her anxiety about whether I could tolerate her neediness, and she would squelch her aggressive, frustrated feelings about me, trying to keep me happy.

These strong maternal longings were often admixed with fatherly delight and excitement. In one session she noted my wearing a red tie—and felt amused by it. Later in the session she talked of flying dreams and her associations to being a little girl standing next to her father as he drove a snappy Oldsmobile with rockets on the sides. She had always been excited by fast cars and auto racing.

"I just always felt safe. Sort of like nothing bad would ever happen as long as he was there. I suppose I still believe that."

"And the excitement and rockets next to your Dad."

(Laughs heartily) "You have this way of making these connections. (laughs and laughs)—there must be something to it or I wouldn't be responding this way."

"Does it seem right?"

" . . . it's hard to put the affective and cognitive together. When you say it, there's a certain warmness. It's like it makes me feel giddy. Like I always associate to my father in terms of excitement and safety, things happening . . . the bright side."

"The giddy feeling you just had now, is that like the feeling you had as a little girl?"

" . . . It's like I always think of myself as being very special to him as a little girl. There wasn't any competition . . . "

"Just you and he in the front seat."

(Laughs giddily) "Right! I don't know what this has to do with a red tie. Maybe it's a way of engaging you."

"My rocket tie."

"Right! (laughs) red rockets, red rockets. . . . "

The Road

Over time a previously unexplored area of her life came to the fore, a dark
and guarded secret, a sexual relationship in college that confused and frightened her still with her experience of wild passion and compulsivity. She had
tried to put it aside, simply not think of it, though its insidious effect still
exerted itself: She felt bad and ashamed.

Only recently had she begun to broach this in her analysis, and it filled her
with trepidation. Reluctantly she began to explore this secret to herself. The
"pathogenic secret" has long been described in the history of psychiatric
literature, certainly before Freud.[4] Its origins are closely attached to sin and
hence religion (and so "confession"). My therapeutic tack, though, was not to
push. Rather than the content of the material itself, I was more interested in
her apprehension for us to explore together.

During this period, she began one session, "I feel like I'm where I've been
so many times before: mildly overwhelmed, I don't know where to start. I'm
anxious."

(I wondered to myself why this was the case. It was a Monday, and that always seemed a harder session for her to begin. Perhaps it connected to our brief
separation, what Freud called the "Monday crust." She needed to re-establish
where I was, to connect with me. Nevertheless, I thought her uncomfortable-
ness might have to do with how she was experiencing me in general. This was
something to be explored: I didn't want to leave it simply accepted as the way
treatment was and had to be.) I replied, "Though it's not clear why you feel that
way, what about me, for example, might make you anxious to explore."

"When you ask, it makes me smile, I've heard you ask so many times . . . it
all remains unclear." (Her affect became lighter, I thought in response to my
merely saying something, to my making contact – as we had noticed before.)

"Saturday night I had this dream of being on a dirt road again." (I had just
asked a question about her experience of me, and she had been left uncertain,
but now we are shifting into a new and symbolic language – and here she is
fluent and articulate.) "I was driving in the country with someone. It wasn't
calm or, as a friend of mine put it recently, it wasn't bucolic . . . it was in
turmoil. Trees were uprooted. There was this field where people were plowing,
turning over the earth. Whoever I was with was driving very fast and I was
frightened." (I say nothing, but I immediately "hear" her as talking about the
treatment [the car] and me [the driver] – that is my mind set. The landscape
itself, fields being plowed, trees being upturned – is this her experience of
what is happening to her in treatment? But I want not to jump in interpreting

what seems evident; I would like to suspend my construction, gather her associations, explore her lived experience, and deepen my own resonance with it. She continues uninterrupted.)

"At one point we went around this curve in the road and this car came in the other direction, a yellow convertible like _____'s (a male psychologist friend). I went around the curve on the wrong side of the road and I thought, 'Oh my god, if that car had been seconds later or we had been seconds earlier we'd have had a head-on collision!'" (Interestingly, only as I am writing these words and re-imagining her dream do I realize that the scene I set up in my mind's eye *as I listened to her then* is very similar to a recollected experience I had as a teenager joy-riding with a friend. He was notoriously reckless and to my surprise [no surprise] he accelerated blindly into a sharp curve on a hill. For a brief moment I had been thrilled and terrified—and later, guilty. My parents had warned me not to get into a car with him. This was the borrowed scenery and affect for my internal, empathic [or projected] landscape.)

"It (the countryside) wasn't ugly or awful—but uprooted and overturned. Nothing was picturesque. I was thinking, what is it with these dirt roads? I wasn't in the forest, more in the country, with fields, hilly." (This, I thought, is where she spent summers growing up; it is a childhood landscape. I wondered about the other person, and asked.)

"I don't know who it was; I assume it was a man . . . the thing I remember most is wanting him to slow down. . . . " She moved on to the lack of calm or peace in her life, the turbulence at work and at home (and, in this sense, the dream captures a pervasive feeling about her life).

"In your dream," I ask, "what was your feeling as you looked at the landscape?"

"What's going on here?—it was this question. It sort of made me shudder; it was creepy. The fields that were being plowed were—it doesn't make any sense at all—vineyards, which I associate to childhood." (I did not catch on here until later: Vineyards are not plowed.)

As I listened to her, my internal image of her dream was revising itself into a dreary and frightening place, and so I asked, "In the dream, I don't know if you would know, but what was the weather like?"

She laughed and answered, "Oh. I *do* know! It was *gray*. And cold. It was more like spring, but gray and cold, sort of like this morning. It wasn't wet, but the sun wasn't shining." (This is the setting of the dreamscape: a cold, gray spring day—and how much better it captures her frame of mind than any of our professionally descriptive words, like "dysphoria"!)

Her affect here intensifies to being urgent and upset. "And it was like things wouldn't stop. If I looked to my right they were plowing these fields and, if I looked, it was disorienting. And going very fast. And on my left trees were uprooted and like nothing would stop. And nothing was peaceful and I want something peaceful and nothing would stop and like there were no brakes. It's not like out of control, but like, isn't anything *pretty*? (Here she starts to cry softly.) Like it all had the potential, but it wasn't there for one reason or another (and she cries). It also felt — it wasn't as if I was in a strange land — it all felt very familiar. Sort of like as if I'd been there before. . . . I sort of felt like I'm stuck there in my mind. I sort of feel I can't get the scene out of my head: These vineyards being plowed on one side and these trees uprooted on the other. I don't know what the thing was about uprooted trees."

Her affect is intense and alive in this striking image, and so I ask, "What did they look like?"

"Well, it's funny. What comes to mind now is like this small hillside that's not a lot of trees, not a forest. (She laughs.) What I was struggling with: uprooted trees, sometimes walking in the woods and seeing these gigantic trees and the *whole base is exposed*. And it's sort of creepy and (laughs) even fascinating, this whole underworld. I've moved to feeling sad to just thinking about those trees. And I can remember times standing in the woods looking at trees that had fallen over and all these intertwining roots and all this *dirt* and everything is crawling around, and how everything is intertwined. Sort of like a maze. You don't usually see all of that, sort of under the earth."

"Buried," I say.

"Right," she laughs heartily. "Obviously I am thinking about myself! Things that I keep buried. How scary it is to sort of expose these things: It's scary and creepy and *exciting* all at the same time, intriguing (sighs) . . . I've seen a huge gigantic tree come crashing to the ground. To actually see it unearthed and the fascination of looking at it. Here the process of talking about things — it's so scary and frightening. Afterwards I can think about it and look at it. But it's still frightening. I was thinking about what I talked about last week, that business about my secret love. It is still unresolved and it's more than unpleasant, it's awful and difficult. It's hard to talk about. At the same time I can try to think about it and look at my life as a whole and try to put it into some intellectual perspective. What's at its base, what are the roots of it all (laughs) — and I'm not so sure I want to look at it."

(At this point, she has latched onto the dream images, metamorphosing them into metaphor and playfully giving them meaning. Nevertheless, she is intellectualizing the image, removing herself from the lived experience and providing closure. Interpersonally, she is engaging me as well, perhaps even placating me [or slowing me down].) I decide to re-enter the dream image as a way of exploring and clarifying these complex possibilities: "Do you remember your feelings and your sense of the driver?"

(She laughs.) "No — but I just had a near escape from *death*. The yellow convertible, what a crazy driver he was, more than the person I was with. We negotiated the curve, but the other guy was crazy."

"You couldn't or didn't tell the driver to slow down?"

"Oh, I think so. Oh yes — but it didn't do any good."

"He didn't listen?"

"No. That was part of the problem. And everything was happening so fast and everywhere I looked, left or right, things were uprooted, upturned. The scenes would never stop. . . . "

(I decide to comment on the dream as relating to me and her treatment.) "You know, when you came in today, I raised that old question of why you might be afraid of me. It's clear in the dream you feel I'm going too fast." (Spence [1982] would explicate that this is a construction on my part, that, as Viderman [1979] has described, I have created something through my own association to her dream, "that something may become true simply as a consequence of being stated." Havens [1984], following Austin's work [1962] refers to something very similar, "performative speech.")

"I understand that connection — maybe that's what I am saying. If you were to ask that straight out (laughs) I'd say everything is just fine, but it makes me think! . . . I ask myself: 'Do I feel that way?' Funny, I always feel that I'm not going fast enough, that I should go faster (laughs sarcastically) so I can keep up with you!" (falls silent)

(She seems to be confirming my comment that she feels I go too fast. Nevertheless, have I taken her dream image and simply molded it to give us a new language to talk about this aspect of our relationship? Am I in the inscape, or creating it? Are we creating it together?)

Referring to her laughing, I remark: "Jokes can hide a lot." (I might have acknowledged here that she must have felt that the jokes and playfulness were necessary with me: Hiding her anger is a way of protecting our relationship if she felt I might not tolerate her expression of it.)

(Laughs heartily) "I thought, I can't believe I just said that. I was lying here in surprise, like, 'What I just say?! . . . hmm.'" (longish silence)

"Editing?" (A shorthand word for us, meaning she is censoring out what she feels she can say to me.)

"How'd you guess? (laugh). I was just thinking about your interpretation and if I felt you were going too fast, and then my comment. I was sort of left with it, resonating. Sort of wondering, is that what I was struggling with? There's some sort of good feeling there. I always feel that at some moments of truth or clarity, I laugh, whenever you say something that feels right or quite right on, that it hits some chord. How I laugh! There is probably also some anxiety."

Later, reflecting on joy riding, the yellow convertible, my own high school memory, her memories of her father's rocket car, and my rocket tie (from a previous session), I return to the dream image: "You know I was thinking that at other times you've described going fast as exhilarating."

Excitedly, "Oh! It is! (sigh) But it's one thing going fast in control and another going fast when out of control. I sometimes like going fast. But I wasn't driving the car. It has to do with whether I feel safe — not even control, but whether I feel safe . . . "

Paradise Lost: The Office

As the treatment deepened, themes of separation and loss intensified. What seemed to me to be small perturbations in our relationship — weekends, my vacations, or variations from the expected routine — were for my patient major events; she was constantly vigilant to me and my potential loss. Prior to my being away for a week she had a horrific dream. She was watching her mother hold her baby sister. In an instant the baby's throat was slit/exploded, and shit oozed out.

I had been planning to change the physical structure of my office for some time; construction was timed for my summer vacation. The changes in my office preoccupied her: Would she feel protected? Where would she be? Where would I be? What would the space be like? Would she be able to locate me? She had dreams about being lost in space, unable to connect to me: Where was I? Moments of doom plagued her.

Taste and smell were often the predominant sensory experiences in her dreamscapes. Immediately prior to my vacation she had two dreams that were unpleasant and distressing to her. In one she was sucking at her own breasts — and they were dry and awful tasting. The day after the dream, her neck was stiff and aching.

(S)MOTHERING

> For people could close their eyes . . . to horrors, to beauty, and their ears to melodies or deceiving words. But they could not escape scent. For scent was a brother of breath. Together with breath it entered human beings, who could not defend themselves against it, not if they wanted to live. And scent entered into their very core, went directly to their hearts, and decided for good and all between affection and contempt, disgust and lust, love and hate.
> —PATRICK SÜSKIND (1986)

In a second dream her mother was a baby with a diaper full of shit. The dominant sensory experience was olfactory and spatial: a shit-reeking, small space — she felt overpowered and unable to breathe.

She had developed her asthma as a teenager, at a time when her mother seemed particularly unbearable. Now she was reliving earlier spaces—the suffocating, drowning, life-draining experience of her mother. Open space is air, freedom, and father. These bodily sensations had become an organizing lived experience for her in the world, beyond metaphor. Freud (1900) recorded the apparent prescient dream experiences of some physical illnesses, like congestive heart failure, that first manifest themselves in the body, the unconscious, as sensations of smothering. Every physician knows the sign: "I can't breathe and I go sit by the window for fresh air." Open space—wind—being able to breathe, *the inscape changes first, before awareness.*

In retrospect, the effect of the office changes seems inevitable. She flew into a rage with me; her expression of it was sudden, total, and unlike the intellectualized intimations of anger in previous sessions. She could barely talk, and wanted to hurt me. I had taken something away, something had been irrevocably lost. The experience was not then felt by her as symbolic; it was actual and tangible: I had removed the textures from the office and she was bereft and in a fury!

And this I had not appreciated. My own experience was to open up my working space; I wanted light. Was this because of my predominantly visual orientation to the world? But to her I had destroyed the textures. The carpet had been replaced by one with a lower pile; the grass-cloth wallpaper was gone and the wall painted; the rug wall hanging moved to the floor—the effect, the feel, disappeared for her.

The space had been violated, too. The smaller, darker, intimate enclosure was lost into the abyss of space. Where was I? I had been the good mother, the lost or never-had mother, the mother she longed for—and I had taken that mother (that is, myself) away. And was I now the depriving, hateful mother? The good feeling we had shared vanished, and the intensity of her rage felt overpowering and scary to her.

And there was intense bodily pain, new to her: Her eyes literally hurt to take in the sight of our devastated space; she felt a physical pain that she was sure was in her heart. And she wanted to hurt me in revenge. She wanted to take permanent markers to the walls and destroy the visual changes. She had a dream of a puppy urinating all over a couch. If only she could make me suffer as she had . . . and though on one level she hated to draw any insight from these reactions (it was what I would want), she persisted.

These predominantly survival concerns had a triangular quality to them. During this period she dreamt of my wife being run over by train, removed from the scene, and acknowledged that she thought some of the office changes must surely have been because of my wife's input. She had dreams of my wife leaving me. When I commented that that would leave just us two, she remarked with a laugh, "That would be nice."

Only a year later did I learn that the color I had chosen for my office matched that of her childhood home.

Acknowledging

My silence felt awful, but anything I said pained her, as if I were pulling at the wound. What could I do? — there was no going back, the office was changed. I thought I had appreciated her pain at what I had done, but this was not her experience. What was I missing that left her feeling unacknowledged? In retrospect the moment this acknowledgment came about seems mundane and anticlimactic. There were of course many precursor moments, but here it clicked.

She was quietly grieving and brooding.

"I feel . . . apathetic, passive, walked over and walked on. Not valued, not counted, not respected."

"That I have not respected you in making the office changes."

"I've been thinking about and thinking about it. The business about the office is there all the time. I wake up and don't know if I dreamt about it . . . it's just there. I can struggle and struggle and nothing will happen."

"What would you like me to do?"

"Thank you for asking . . . (sobs and sobs and sobs) . . . That's the first time you've asked me what I'd like (sobs and then laughs). Last night I kept thinking you said you didn't understand. There are so many levels. That you didn't understand, what's gone or the change is like how important it all was to me the way it was. . . . You kept wanting to go past it . . . to understand. . . . I'd like to move the couch back . . . the rug. . . . I can't ever get back what's lost. . . . You're saying, what can I do, acknowledges in a different way than 'let's understand.' I was jealous . . . thinking: Oh, this is such a nice space — and why isn't it nice for me?"

The cloud lifted.

Ironically I had talked about understanding and this had left her feeling deeply misunderstood. She was right: understanding not only avoided her affect and distanced me from her pain, but was also my subtle way of reality-testing her feelings as if they were an overreaction to what I had done. I was imposing my point of view on hers.

In retrospect, would I have done things differently (for example, not changed my office)? No, nor did she expect that. Paradoxically, in her feeling that I now really understood what she must have felt as a result of what I'd done, that what I do can hurt her deeply, she moved away from her former position (and me, mine). Curiously, as I empathize with her, she empathizes with me — she understands my reality — and now her own reality changes with respect to me. Reality-testing takes on a new significance, a sharing of mutual perspectives and a deepening awareness of our own contributions to the spiral of meaning. (I will explore these notions further in Chapters 7 and 8.)

For my patient other feelings began to tumble out. She dreamt of vast cavernous spaces, black voids, pregnant women, being lost. She felt immensely relieved that she had not driven me away with her anger.

"I think I was *scared*. My association was to leaving a very young child in a very strange place—they just shriek. They're terrified. That's the way it felt for me. Like 'O my God! What do I do now?' I didn't feel safe. . . . Why do I respond to my terror with anger? . . . I imagine being totally alone with nothing around me in this total void and left screaming, just screaming. And nothing to hang on to and nobody hears me. Just there. And I have this image of standing in the playpen screaming and screaming and being totally ignored and then falling asleep."

In a later session I say, "You had this image of an infant."

"A child, two years or less."

"But no one answering, no voice."

"And that's what's so different here. The response (cries)—it is *so*. It's *so*. It feels so good, and yet I don't even know how to integrate it . . . it's like I'm alive."

"That implies that you weren't alive."

" . . . it does imply. (laughs) I just noticed a flower [in the office] *growing*."

A month later—

"You kept talking—I needed that—to know that you were there. And I could feel it. What was most helpful . . . is just hearing your voice. And I would say to myself, 'It's going to be OK.' If you had thrown me out it would have validated my feeling bad. What you did was essentially to hold me through this big temper tantrum. Hold me in place, which was exactly what I needed. Allowing me to have it but holding me there. I felt I never could have gotten as angry as I did without feeling safe. It felt very safe, but I would leave here and feel it was all gone. That there was nothing good that was left (cries), and I didn't want to be stuck there with all that anger. I wanted it to go away, but it wouldn't. I just remember when you asked me what it was that I'd like that was a turning point . . . "

The therapist and patient need to discover and rediscover for themselves basic truths. Heinz Kohut contributed so much to the comprehension of the very kind of experience my patient and I lived through: Disintegration anxiety secondary to the disruption of selfobject ties is the most profound anxiety one can suffer (1984). Baker and Baker (1987) nicely summarize: What is feared is not physical death but the loss of humanness, or psychological death. These inevitable disruptions of selfobject ties to the therapist, or empathic "failures," "must be acknowledged by the therapist, who must accept his or her contribution (however unintended or impossible to avoid). . . . We cannot overemphasize that, if the bond is genuinely reestablished, the very intensity of the disruption indicates that the therapeutic process is working as it should" (p. 5). By acknowledgment I mean the affirmation of the other's point of view as central and valid versus the imposition of one's own assertions of truth, that is, a stance of continuing to search for the other's experience. Evelyne Schwaber (1981, 1983), in particular, has provided a valuable theoretical framework for the systematic understanding and use of acknowledgment in the subtle interaction of patient and therapist, that is to say, empathy as a mode of listening and conveyance of listening.

One Last Hug: The Breasts

Fragment of a session a few months later:

"This morning I awoke at 5 o'clock — thinking about this office. I had been thinking over the weekend that I found it soothing. I was thinking about flowers and the colors of the cushions, and the rug and how they all sort of blend together."

"Bet you thought you'd never say that."

"Does sound a little strange, doesn't it? (laughs heartily) How did I get there, to this spot. My next association is to the saddest story I heard from a nurse friend; it brought tears to my eyes. There had been a patient who died on the ward, a woman with an eight year old son. The son was sobbing, just sobbing and one of the staff went over and held him. In the morning the woman had been thrashing around and they had tied her arms down, and they were still tied down at the time she had died. (Now she starts crying softly.) It makes me so anxious. And this little boy went over and untied them (cries) and told his mother he wanted one last hug and took his mother's arms and wrapped them around him (cries) . . . "

"It's heartbreaking."

"(Cries) It really is. It stirs up so much feeling in me, the pain of it. Yeah, it's heartbreaking. It's interesting I associate to it after talking of this room, this office, this space."

. . .

"How do you experience the space now?"

"Funny, I remember how I used to talk about the wallpaper [that used to be] and the various shades of light in it. The other day I was thinking about the walls now and the change in colors it has in different lights. Sometimes the walls seem different colors, sometimes the same. I sometimes go back to the way it was. When I'm not here and I think about the office, I always think about the part I'm not in—over there." (She points to the wicker couch she used to sit on in my waiting room; it no longer fit in the new waiting room and I had moved it into the present office.) "I wonder if someday I'll just come in and sit on that couch, just to be there."

"One last hug."

"Yeah . . . " (then silent)

"The story you told—"

"Oh! (Her affect is now very sad.) Yeah, I want to sit there and put my hands between the cushions. Somedays . . . I'd sit there (in the waiting room) and put my hands between the cushions and it felt so nice and so soft. Sometimes I'd feel them, and run my hands across the fabric—I miss that."

(Something flickers in my consciousness: I have experienced that sensation with her in the past as she had described it. I *know* that feeling from *her* description, *I have a memory from within her world of memory.* Of course it is my internal representation of her world, but I "remember" the resonant tactile feeling of a memory of hers when she was quite small. *I have lived it in empathy*; I am certain of this.) I remark, "You once said that you had a pillow that—"

"Yes," she completes my thought. "I remember." (Havens uses this finishing of sentences as a test of whether one is in empathy [1978a, 1978b]. How complex it is here and how natural: She empathizes with my empathizing with her—and moves on to elaborate her experience; we are in synchrony. I will further take up the notion of empathy with oneself through the other in Chapter 7.) "I used to imagine with the pillow that that's how my mother's breast would feel. And I remember having that association when I came in here. My mother's pillow was satiny with foam in it. I'd open it up and feel it. It was quite satisfying. Like your wall-hanging, I wanted to put my fingers on it, to feel it . . . "

"Your dead mother." (Should I have said this? She was talking about me and her mother and being soothed—and I was shifting away. Moreover, my statement is jarring [just like her mother, recall her dream about my mother and her own] and symbolic: Her mother is not really dead, but she has seemed dead and deadening. I am creating a new thought. My reasoning at the time: the most intense feelings of this session had been with the story of the little boy saying good-bye to his dead mother; it had been heartrending. I was trying to return to that unbearable feeling. Now I wonder if was I getting away from the intense feelings about me and her wanting to touch.)

"Ummm, hmmm. (laughs) It's funny you say that, I don't even have a response. It's not sad, more matter of fact. . . . Was it ever different? That boy was eight; eight was when my sister was born, and I associate that with my grandfather's death and things sort of *declining.* . . . I really don't recall things. I don't recall my mother's presence . . . more the presence of my grandmother and aunt. I have these associations to wandering around by myself. I don't remember being part of a family. I can't recall things I did with my mother . . . the weekends I went to my grandmother's and I spent time with my aunt. They're dead, too."

"You were orphaned more than once in your life."

She sighs heavily. "I've never used the word in relation to myself. It seems to fit. Funny, I had a dream about my aunt recently. I'd been in a store and had seen little tins with coal in them. And that night I had a dream of a truck loaded with coal. My aunt was killed by her car skidding on ice and she had a head-on collision with a truck loaded with coal. She was a very significant person to me. . . . "

It turns out, this aunt was a highly significant person to her, and one whom we had never really talked about. This aunt had been the antithesis of her mother and had provided a sense of vitality. My patient had been very attached to her aunt and had always avoided grieving her loss. But this is not yet where she was in the treatment. I had pushed open a door, and I had a glimpse of this aspect of her inscape, but we were not to return to this until much later. Now I am reminded of her message to me in the speeding car dream: She needed to go down other roads first and at her own speed.

Stairways in the Dark

> And we thank Thee that darkness reminds us of light.
>
> —T.S. ELIOT

The following is a fragment of a subsequent session and begins with a dream: "I'd come here . . . and you weren't here. I laid down on the couch, except it was so dark. And I kept trying to turn on the lights, except none of them worked. I'd feel along the walls, but none of the switches worked. I tried to adjust my eyes to the darkness except they never did; it was just dark. . . . I could hear your voice on the other side of the wall. I was frightened that you'd come in and it'd still be dark — like what if you couldn't find the light either?"

"And there were blankets on the couch, and I pulled them up. . . . I didn't like the feeling much. I wasn't panicked, but I was getting pretty exhausted. The other thought was there was another room on my left, and it was pretty dark, too. There was a staircase going into that room. I just woke up."

With trepidation she had witnessed her increasing dependency on me at a time of much unhappiness in her life, and the dream captured that general sense of things. Her constant fear was that I would grow tired of her and would abandon her, shut her out, and this too was evident in the experience of the dream. I was cut off from her, unavailable, and she was left alone and frightened. Light is clarity and safety, a symbol for insight, en-lighten-ment, and hope — could I disperse the darkness? Had I, too, lost my way in the murkiness? Black is indeterminate space in which the presence of another can be uncertain and tenuous. Moreover, the other can hide or leave. Black is a psychological space in which one finds the other through sound, groping, and touch. Would she be left alone to soothe and care for herself?

Awakening, she has fled the dreamscape, as if to avoid its dormant potential and what was to come next. Frustration and anxiety hang over the dream. She is left with that image of the staircase reaching into a mysterious space, creating an unresolved tension, like that of an unknown and incomplete musical phrase, suspended, dangling . . .

Steps create a way in and a way out, a trap or an escape. They are both separations and connections, lower to higher, between two spaces. They are in between, transitional, a change; one passes through a staircase to something else. Jung saw them as symbolic of the spiritual; Freud saw them as sexual motifs (that is, the activity in climbing). For small children, steps are exciting and dangerous, a physical challenge to master. Interpersonally they are also a warning and a hope — children listen in the night for our steps. The steps, as presented in this present narrative, are something incomplete, unknown, unexplored.

Her very next associations after the staircase were to violence, a gangster movie. Later in the session she elaborated a stunningly sadistic image from the film, and nervously laughed.

Her associative drift moved toward recent moments of confusion, for example, coming out of a movie theater on a summer day and finding that a freak New England storm had left ice in her yard. In another dream she watched a baptism at a distance and wanted to cross over a lake. There was a Pied Piper (me in the transference?). She thought of her mother and a recent conversation that had left her feeling frustrated and tense. She returned to the staircase dream, her confusion about it, and its disconcerting quality.

I am aware that we are both confused, that it is difficult (and necessary) for her (and me) to stay with the anxiety, that I too want understanding and light. We are hungry for meaning; perhaps meaning is our way of connecting — this, too, I know must be taken up. It is complex to me. Any meaning I give is not in a vacuum — we create a meaning together, always. "You were waiting for me, hoping I'd turn on the light."

"I wanted you to be there because then it would be safe. I felt myself alone in the dark, feeling the walls, switches, and nothing happens."

(Should I have stayed here, with this complex state of mind and interaction with me, that she feels I have been unavailable?) "You described a staircase."

"I don't know where it went. Another room with a huge archway. Dark, more like an entrance hall. The staircase went upstairs, but I don't know where . . . thinking about the staircase. The house where I was born, my aunt and uncle's [father was away in the armed services]. One of the few places where my cousins and I would play was on the staircase . . . it was away from traffic, quiet and we'd play. The staircase in the dream was like that, natural wood, dark, three stairs and a landing, then a right turn and up some more. Funny, those stairs, the carpet had metal rods to hold it in place, one doesn't see them anymore."

(Now the mysterious dream staircase had become connected to a staircase in memory. Perhaps here we could pick up a thread. Paradoxically, I am trying to deepen my sense of her confusion, to immerse myself in it, to feel what it connects with in her life's experience. There is a present confusion, but it connects with a larger confusion and uncertainty, her particular world view of confusion with its own elaborate history.) "Where did the staircase go?"

"There were two bedrooms on the second floor, that's where my mother slept when I was born. I slept on the porch, which was all enclosed. . . . " She had often wondered why she had been left on the porch, alone.

(I am reminded of her recurring image of a young child shrieking into the void.) "When you were very little and were afraid in the dark, the stairways led to your mother . . . "

"In the dream that was out of reach."

. . .

"In your dream you hoped for me to come in."

"Yes, but you were next door talking to your wife."

"That's a new detail."

(Laughs) "I didn't mention that before?! Oh, hmm, interesting that I didn't include that. I can't stand it. This is exhausting."

She becomes tired (as in the dream) and now sad. "It's like, 'Oh, I can't have you either' . . . "

Clearly she had been experiencing me as unreachable and her associations reached down, through the dream image of the staircase, into her experience of her mother, into an atmosphere of rage, longing, and fear. I understood later in the treatment her fear of understanding itself—she would lose me if she got better. In a sense this was enacted around the dream sequence: Being in the dark was safe as long as we were together, but I pushed into a new and unknown space, and she lost me.

The dream staircase began with me, led to another staircase in a different space (one in memory) of her mother, and from there to the earliest circumstances of her life (a screen memory, a space not so clear, one in the misted glass of intellect, memory, conjecture, body—an almost-memory). And then she returns to our space in the present, together, a space threatened and unreal, a space vulnerable to the other spaces that I live in.

Postscript

In later stages of the analysis, sexual fantasies were to emerge with vitality and joy. She had vivid fantasies of being my three-and-a-half year-old daughter. Thinking of me, she had bought a card of a cute, sexy little girl who was naked and standing on a couch, peering over the back of it. She recalled being four, five, six years old and alone with her father, swimming and feeling beautiful and loved. She wished she could keep me to herself, and recalled being a child and proudly possessive of her father. But these strivings had then felt dangerous. She recalled being afraid of her mother and of mother's chasing her with a knife. Mother had been beautiful as a younger woman; my patient became aware of an empathy with mother's becoming depressed and trapped within her life. Mother's plight plagued her—as a daughter she had no choice but to escape. Her aunt, seldom mentioned (see the coal truck story above), had been of "incredible importance" to her growing up and emerged as someone with whom the young girl identified. Slowly her life seemed to become her own—and with new feeling and passion.

Reading over these notes, I realize in retrospect that much of the empathic interaction, excitement and discovery was to pull her away from the more intolerable experience of bearing her depression. In a broad sense I represented the promise of father's playfulness, his aliveness. Her fear was of some deep identification with mother, who was deadness and emptiness, and my silence (re)created a panic. It was only over time that this deadness could be plumbed and borne—and this was the work of the next phase. I do not feel critical of the first phase in this regard; it was how we established a relationship and how we came to grasp one aspect of her inner life and inscape. But a more difficult part of her world awaited us. The experience was deader—but no less real. Insight trails experience.

With these vignettes I am struck that, like the staircase dream, there is a sense of incompleteness. There is no clear narrative here—and I feel as if I owe the reader lucidity, a working out to completion. Maybe I should edit out points of theoretical contention and not embarrass myself with the evidence of my actual remarks, that is, that I might now do things otherwise. I want the comfort of a pure and steady stance—or at least the illusion of a clear vision.

Sheldon Roth recently remarked (1987), "In a diagnostic interview, or an extended consultation one can have a brief moment of glory in the sun—you seem like a sage—but once we dig in for the long haul, attempting to effect change, all the frailties, vagueness, and unclarity of the participants and the technique come to the fore. . . . Clinical experience is otherwise."

Empathy, too, is otherwise — brief moments of certainty amidst Keats's sea of "irritable reaching after fact & reason." It is only after the treatment is over that we look back in clarity, tranquility, and with regret or reassurance.

Persephone's Two Worlds

A clinical moment occurs to me, one that captures an essence of this particular treatment and anticipates the chapters to follow.

During a week before I was to be away for a summer vacation my patient dreamt of an abandoned greenhouse, the windows clouded with grime, and the flowers and plants withered and dead. Prior to the dream her associative drift had been to death and the loss of dear friends. Now it went to the green house window in my waiting room: The previous year the plants had been removed the day before I was to leave — and she remembered her desolation.

It was not only that I might die or leave her in grief but that without me she felt dead inside: I was the center of her life, her raison d'etre. Without me her world became suspended into the coldness of an internal winter, numb and waiting.

Persephone comes to mind, daughter of Demeter, the yellow haired goddess of corn and the harvest. Stolen away by Hades, lord of the underworld and king of the dead, Persephone's plight was to be of two worlds, in the dark land of the dead for half of the year and then with her beloved mother amidst the living. Persephone comes alive and dies in the eternal cycle of the seasons, the world reflecting her own misery or happiness as she greens into life and fades into deadness. Her existence ripped in two, she is always anticipating. Even in her gaiety there is sorrow for the evanescence of her happiness.

Persephone seems particularly relevant at this juncture — she embodies my patient's lived experience of starkly contrasting and alternating inscapes. In the next chapter I explore the notion of world view, its inertia and embeddedness in the interpersonal, the problem of centeredness, and the use of the other as raison d'etre. Later, in the search for the interior life of the other and the center that experiences, I turn to the problem of the split self and discontinuous states, empathy with oneself and the interpersonal spiral of meaning.

PART IV
Imagining the Self

"A day of dappled seaborne clouds."
The phrase and the day and the scene
harmonized in a chord. Words. Was
it their colours? He allowed them to
glow and fade, hue after hue; sunrise
gold, the russet and green of apple
orchards, azures of waves, the grey-
fringed fleece of clouds. No, it was
not their colours; it was the poise
and balance of the period itself. Did
he love the rhythmic rise and fall of
words better than their associations
of legend and colour? Or was it that,
being as weak of sight as he was shy
of mind, he drew less pleasure from
the reflection of the glowing sensible
world through the prism of a language manycoloured and richly
storied than from the contemplation
of an inner world of individual emotions mirrored perfectly in a lucid
supple periodic prose.

—JAMES JOYCE

CHAPTER 6

Reflections on World View

We see the lives of others through lenses of our own grinding . . . they look back on ours through ones of their own.

—CLIFFORD GEERTZ

I n this chapter I will gather together some assumptions about world view that relate to the process of empathy. In particular I will examine the inherent mass of a world view, its inertia or resistance to change. We distinguish this in its myriad forms — for example, symptom formation and repetition compulsion — but these seemingly discrete manifestations of psychic life achieve their coherency and meaning only within the larger context of articulated world views.

The relativity of the therapist's and patient's point of view one to the other can destabilize fixed perspectives (unless one point of view merely imposes itself on the other). It is this unavoidable disjunction of vistas in the empathic dialogue that is one avenue for change — the ground shifts.

Case Example: A Bubble Bursts

Apparently paranoid and psychotic for many years, a man in his early thirties was admitted to the hospital. A tragic history unfolded to the treatment team. As a youth he had shown great promise: he had been a star athlete, popular and well known, a winner of coveted scholarships. He had married his high-school sweetheart and together they had a daughter whom he dearly loved. All of this fell apart when his wife left him, now many years ago. He simply withdrew and retained almost no contact with the outside world, spending his time quietly grandiose in his room in his parents' home.

He presented as gently cooperative, a nice man despite his paranoia. (How often we see this, an almost child-like simplicity side by side with the suspiciousness [Grunebaum and Perlman, 1973]. This naiveté points to a vulnerability to the predation of others [Havens, 1989] and, I think, often covers a disbelief reflecting some early betrayal. Recent historical evidence about Freud's Schreber paper is a case in point—the "real" childhood abuses were nothing less than astonishing in their ingenuity, the delusions rather mundane in comparison [Niederland, 1959a, 1959b].) Our patient was vigorously treated with antipsychotic medications and, gratifyingly to his caregivers, his mental status soon cleared of its overtly psychotic features. With lucidity and poignancy he talked to his therapist about the loss of his former craziness; he had a longing for his psychotic oblivion. It was, he said, "as if a great bubble had burst." Now it seemed that he was at last coming to grips with his pain and the lost years. And so the staff felt pleased with his progress and started plans for work rehabilitation. Apparently normal for the first time in years, he went home and killed himself in the family garage with carbon monoxide.

Over time my understanding of this series of events has changed. At first I had seen the psychosis as protective, thinking that it must have saved this man from experiencing the unbearable reality of his situation. This, I realized much later, was not quite right.

I had, it seemed, too narrowly conceptualized the idea of "defense." There is a tendency to treat defense as if it were a component of a larger grouped mental apparatus, like a part of an elaborate machine.

What, we still wonder, do we mean by "defense"? Defense against what? Unseen enemies—revealed to us by our theoreticians—jostle and replace one another in their relentless assault against the fortress of the self. Metapsychologically we can stress drives, ego affects, insults to self-esteem, unbearable feelings, awareness of ultimate concerns . . . the list is as long as the number of theoretical positions. Interestingly, such different conceptualizations of the psyche contradict one another as to *what* one defends against—but the idea of defense itself is universally accepted in depth psychologies. Ironically we remain on safer ground with the general notion of a defensive process than we do with specific etiology: The destructive scar tissue signifies a reaction to something that we can only infer. As with some physical disease processes, for example, tuberculosis, it is the defenses themselves that are so ravaging. A synthetic and pragmatic approach would be to take the overview, that is, that each theoretical conceptualization describes a piece of a larger puzzle and each captures a salient element.

No one ever actually experiences a defense per se; we deduce that from the consequences. We infer that defense, like a fever, alerts to an internal struggle of the organism. The lived experience, however, is different and points to a broader significance. The enlightened, compulsive handwasher may *know* that the washing is logically unnecessary, that it is an intrusive symptom (that is, not-me), but in his or her heart the hands are experienced as dirty, contaminated, and the world is a dangerous and infective place.

In the example above the psychosis was more than a defense, it was part of an elaborate solution to the devastation of a universe that had crumbled: It was an alternate world view. (The notion of autism captures this meaning, the turning inward to a protected personal world with the exclusion of troubling external intrusions.) With the dissolution of the psychotic elements a new — and hopeless — world view came to the fore. It was not that "reality" had intervened, but that his assessment of who he was, what his world was, and what it had to offer had changed. Reality itself had changed to that of a different world, less objectively psychotic — but more deadly.

This new world, for example, must have had a different sense of time about it. The old paranoid world view somehow allowed him to suspend himself in time, crystallized in a childhood grandiose present and with perhaps a dreamt of future that would mirror the glory of his past. The protective bubble had burst leaving nothing, no future — worse, no hope of a future. That is, even the future held no possibility of bearable futures. As Havens (1989) has put it, he was nowhere and nowhen. Space, previously both comforting and containing (precariously inside a bubble), as well as expansively grandiose (encompassing the whole world), changed in tandem with time. Now it was a harsher, "realer" space neither protected nor Olympian.

It is not that one illusion had simply replaced the other. Indeed, my assessment of his situation (is my view realer?) was that it was depressingly grim, though I had not seen it as hopeless (and I did not have to live in his skin). In a sense, of course, a world view *can* be defensive against another — why else is one held with such seeming preference and tenacity? My point is that whatever we mean by defensive has to include the pervasiveness of the defense into all areas of the person's life: It is a cognitive style (Shapiro, 1965), a perceptual world view, a way of experiencing time (including present, past, future in their immediate, intermediate, and distant zones); it has a space, color, materiality; it is a manner of peopling the world, a value system. . . . In short, it is part of a coherent, coordinated, and complex personal articulation of one's life.

It seems to me the frequency with which paranoid patients destroy themselves while in an overtly nonpsychotic state speaks to these multiple world views. For many, the paranoid experience presents two alternative life's filters: one magnificently grandiose, the other darkly humiliating. Another patient nostalgically described his past history of paranoia, "I realize I was crazy at those times — but I didn't feel bad." While paranoid he felt important and

strong; nonpsychotic he felt inept, impotent, and ineffectual. Much later this
man, too, killed himself—again a surprise for those who treated him: He had
seemed better, nonpsychotic. From an apparently objective perspective we see
the patient as better, more in touch with reality. But from the patient's perspective, a bubble has burst, and the new inscape is unendurable.[1]

Particularly with psychotic illness one notices abrupt swings in world
views. This is most dramatically apparent with manic-depressive illness, where
such shifts are nothing less than stunning. Even seemingly enduring traits that
one first interprets as character while the undiagnosed patient remains depressed take on a new meaning with the switch into mania, when the external
observer realizes just how state dependent some aspects of personality really
are. True, these switches often point to deep underlying commonalities (the
changes, though 180 degrees, are still on the same axis: soaring self-impor-
tance is the converse of worthlessness). This is merely to say that the person
has limited options. The oscillations of world view are consistent along an
internal plane, be it a central conflict or affective poles: The kernel of one
world view lies within the other, the despair behind the hope; this particular
hope is born of this particular despair, "I might be great" resides in "I might be
nothing." But to the patient and the observer the *feel*, the lived life, is so very
different in the two opposing states.

Usual definitions of psychosis include the loss of the capacity to recognize
reality. This implies that an objective reality gives way to a more subjective,
solipsistic reality. From the patient's point of view, however, there can only be
subjective reality. "Observing ego" admits the consideration of alternative
realities possible to the person, that one is able to step back from subjective
experience and transcend or step to one side of it. It is important to note that
my use here of the term "observing ego" is not in its usual sense of "ability to
see reality." I am suggesting something different: that is, the "recursive ego,"
the ability to move out of the frame, to reflect on self as both subject and
object. Reality in this sense is relative to a point of view, perhaps a more
encompassing one than previously experienced. (I will take this up more fully
in Chapter 8, "Paradox and Possibility.") This recursive quality of self-awareness is crucially important for the working through of a transference regression: One must be able to hold alternative world views simultaneously. Perhaps a necessary part of the meaning of psychosis is the density of subjective
experience; one cannot transcend it or place oneself outside of it; a certain
flexibility of the ego is lost. And perhaps this is why whole nations can appear
psychotic: There can be no observing or recursive ego for those caught up in
the cultural medium. One needs a sense of conflict, contradiction, or alternate
possibility if there is to be a chance of ego transcendence. In a sense, the
whole enterprise of psychotherapy is to open possibilities of new world views;
fundamentally this is what interpretation and working through are all about.

The Feel of Coherency—Me/Not-Me

What makes my world view my own—that is, *me*—and when does it seem *not-me*? What constitutes the feel of a world view? How does one keep it coherent and consistent? These questions are intimately bound up with the concepts of character, the relatively fixed essences of a person's style, as well as with such ideas as syntonic and dystonic. The notion of character, though, has an external emphasis, how the person is experienced by others in the interpersonal.

By the coherency of world view I mean to emphasize the lived experience of familiarity and reliability. That we are internally divided and inconsistent as well I will take up later (see Chapter 8, "Paradox and Possibility"). Interestingly, even in its estrangement, uncanniness, or alien aspects a world view may be consistent; we each have our own particular experience of the strange.

CASE EXAMPLE: PSYCHOSIS SUPERIMPOSED ON PSYCHOSIS—
WHICH MADNESS IS MY OWN?

One patient seen in consultation was impressively psychotic. He was both the devil and god; there was a cosmic conspiracy for his soul; a former girlfriend (dead, I later learned) would someday come back to him as part of the Trinity. He had been admitted not because of his psychosis—which had been longstanding and familiar to everyone—but because of a drug reaction which had been dangerous physically and which had added a toxic psychosis on top of his more chronic schizophrenia. He himself, moreover, knew subjectively that his mind was not now right compared to his own baseline! That is, he could easily differentiate one psychosis from another. What does this mean?

It has been noted that, depending on the exogenous toxin administered, patients with schizophrenia will often be able to distinguish one psychosis from another. For example, a chronically schizophrenic drug abuser can tell the addition of LSD, recognizing that he or she is now tripping. The very inability of schizophrenic patients to make such an identification with the addition of amphetamines has been suggestive evidence for endogenous dopamine as an etiologic factor (Griffith, Cavanaugh, Held, Oates, 1972; Janowsky, El-Yousef, Davis, Sekerke, 1973); that is, amphetamines exacerbate the underlying schizophrenic psychosis rather than introduce a new one.

My point is that psychosis, *even in its very fragmentation of experience*, is a consistent point of view. This is, after all, one of the rationales of the early pioneering efforts in phenomenology for exploring psychopathologic states of mind—there is a coherency of experience. One *lives within* a psychosis. The broad outlines are relatively limited (and hence we can describe syndromes); the individual coloring is, however, always unique.

Correlates of Change in World View

The consistency of world view, as I have explored in earlier chapters, is manifest in perceptual correlates of experience. To this end, as one changes internally, the lived world, the "external" world itself, changes too. We take most note of these shifts in the therapeutic relationship, that is, transference, which feels "out there" (and with an observing ego and insight one learns that it comes from within). But, of course, the entire inner world itself changes along with the transference and with it the experience of the "outside." In a formal manner one could follow serial Rorschachs in a treatment; more intuitively, we note natural markers along the way. Spontaneous images, spontaneous Rorschachs, reflect the inner reworking, the change in world view.

CASE EXAMPLE: THE CLAW AND THE PRINCE:
CHANGES IN A PLASTER RORSCHACH

A patient who was working through a grief-filled ambivalence toward his long dead mother regularly observed the figure of a descending claw-like hand in the plaster swirls of the walls of my office. In a previous therapy he had gotten to painful feelings of anger and resentment toward his mother, but when he terminated that otherwise helpful treatment he was left with an arid memory of her, his love for her replaced with an angry emptiness. He had deeply loved his mother, but always felt that his own aspirations had been thwarted in his effort to please and achieve for her what his unsuccessful father had never been able to provide. Despite his professional success, he had, in a sense, never been able to escape her grip on him; she held onto him even from the grave. The hold, of course, was a consequence of his love for her and her own neurotic and narcissistic caring, which bound him to her as special.

Over time, a serene pastoral cow image spontaneously emerged and coexisted in the plaster Rorschach, and the claw image receded and then disappeared. The transference paralleled these images—and his mother's nurturing and giving qualities came alive to him. These rather concrete, simple images contrasted with this man's sophisticated and complex intellectual understandings and gave a forceful visual clarity to his unconscious processes. Women's profiles emerged and his own mother's image was recollected, an image that previously had been obscured to him in memory, perhaps repressed both out of anger and out of love, that is, to protect her from his anger.

At a later point in his treatment he noticed in my carpet the leftover pattern of vacuum cleaner marks radiating from a central point: He saw a sun burst. He associated to Louis XIV, the Sun King—he had been his mother's Son King. Here the oedipal passion and grandiosity emerged, intertwined with the complicated grief at her loss at a time when he was first successfully and compulsively making his way in the world, for her and him together. Swirls in the plaster, lines in a carpet—the projected images were ingenuous and compelling, telling a spontaneous fairy tale as the treatment unfolded. The changes in the images occurred in tandem with changes in the patient's inner life; they marked shifts of psychic structure and reflected a larger change in world view.

A former generation of psychoanalytic workers used such shifts in world view as signs of therapeutic change—their occurrence heralded ego growth or realignments of defensive structures. For example, Ruth Mack Brunswick's (1928) reanalysis of the Wolf Man relies heavily on the quality of the evolution in his dream productions as markers of psychic reorganization. Jung, too, documents such a process (1952). Implicit in such work is the acceptance of the coordinated whole of experience, what I am referring to with such words as inscape and world view.

The Repetition Compulsion Revisited: The Inertia (Mass) of World View

What keeps a world view stable? Clinical work begins with symptoms, problems, and so our work and literature skew toward the pathological. The question mutates to "What keeps a symptom stable?" The redefined question raises a vexing puzzle about human nature: Why do people hold onto pain and misery? Why are we repetitively masochistic? We give it a name, repetition compulsion, and the name takes on a certain conceptual stability, a repetition compulsion itself in our thinking and our writing (Spence, 1982). This redefinition, pragmatic in its origins, can obscure the larger contextual entanglement of symptoms within a life.

We want to know about such self-inflicted suffering and what keeps it running. Is the repetition compulsion like a motor with its own internal energy propelling it in endless cycles? Freud used this analogy to explain in drive psychological terms the workings of the enigma; the motor turns repetitiously on itself, mechanically, driven and mindless (that is, out of consciousness). The early language of metapsychology lent itself to such a conception; this was "an expression of the most general character of the instincts, namely, their conservatism" (Laplanche and Pontalis, 1973, p. 78). The phenomenon of the repetition compulsion remained problematic, and so the theory continued to evolve, to accommodate. Bibring (1943) was later to distinguish the ego's attempt at restitution, independent of the repetitive tendency of the id. A thorough review of the concept would include the role of trauma, masochism, and the recreation of object relationships.

From an interpersonal perspective Horney (1939) criticized Freud, arguing that his formulations remained too intrapsychic and autonomous in conception. The repetition compulsion is embedded in the social world of one's own making, and it is this inherent circularity of self-fulfilling expectations within the interpersonal that gives the repetition compulsion its motor. The inner compulsion is actualized externally in the reactions of others, which then validates the inner expectations. This idea, of course, was already implicit in Freud's centralization of the transference as the focal point of psychoanalytic treatment: The inner became the outer in the therapeutic relationship itself. More recent psychoanalytic workers (for example, Sandler, 1976) describe enactments in the analytic dialogue, the mutual molding of behavior. Horney (1937, 1950), though, along with Sullivan (1953a, 1956), first pushed the notion of transference to its limits in the interpersonal and social configuration.

The inertia of symptoms becomes then the inertia of the larger mass of world view, like the visible surface of a glacier inexorably sculpting its own bed. "Repetition" is only repetition in the sense that it must repeat; the sheer mass of the system resists change. World view plots its own direction; the possibilities available are limited given its structure. A gyroscope comes to mind, a motor drawing energy from outside itself to create its functional mass, internally spinning and resisting change, providing its own center of gravity, an internal compass.[2]

CASE EXAMPLE: LINGUISTIC SYNCHRONY

> *Everyone has his own way of being betrayed, as*
> *he has his own way of catching cold.*
> —MARCEL PROUST

In the early phases of a treatment a young man felt exceedingly grateful to me. After years of frustration and fear his life had been transformed. He was delighted to be in therapy and experienced me in a very positive way.

At the end of one session he came to an insight about his acting-out destructively towards his boss in a competitive and rivalrous fashion. I added that there were connections to some recent events in treatment and some unexpressed feelings about me.

The next day he was furious with me, complaining that I had my own agenda, that I hadn't given credit to his insights but had been quick to add my own in an implicit criticism. He was sick of this kind of behavior, so much like his wife's and particularly his mother's. He had seldom criticized or been angry with me; now he was in a tirade. It didn't seem I knew what I was doing, I didn't appreciate how hard he was working in the treatment, how important it was to him. I indicated that I realized now that my comment at the end of the previous session had felt devaluing to him. His intense affect lasted most of that hour, but did not continue into the next.

He seemed a different man to me in that session, haughty and condescending — a side of his character that I had not experienced before. At times in that session I found him surprisingly annoying and in a rather unique and irritating way. This was new. Interested in this change (and my own response to it), I wrote in my notes at the time: "testy, adhesive, haughty. . . . " I casually thought about my own choice of words, noting that "adhesive" was an odd term to describe someone, and that on hospital wards I first heard it used to describe the intermorbid personality of some people with temporal lobe epilepsy (Geschwind, personal communication). I had always thought the term to be creative and, in my own experience with some patients so afflicted, to capture an essence. Nevertheless, I did not (and do not) think this man has temporal lobe epilepsy; this was something else. I would have perhaps forgotten about the incident except for events of the next session.

During the subsequent meeting, in the midst of an excited description of an upcoming vacation, he thought of his mother's request that he come see her along the way: "What a downer! She's not intrusive, she's adhesive . . . "

There it was, that peculiar word. Now I better understood. My experience of him had been uncannily similar to his experience of his mother (and of me — had I enacted this relationship? To him, of course, I had). I was now able to experience from an empathic vantage point having lived through an intensely similar experience with him. Roles had been reversed unconsciously in a brief recapitulation of a central relationship.

Had he ever used the term adhesive before to describe his mother? I don't think so, though it would be interesting to study in detail how two people verbally shape the behavior of one another and how this might reveal itself as "empathic understanding" as they become increasingly in synchrony. This would reflect linguistic aspects of the inner constellation of identifications, the object world, the circularity of identifications, the reversal of roles, and the embeddedness of expectations in the interpersonal matrix. With the anecdote just described there had been an extended empathic process, the kind of empathy that comes not only with *projecting* oneself *into* another's world view, but through a sustained *living with* someone, Semrad's empathy of "body time." Together we were creating a language, a shared subjective world experience.

The submerged or as yet unrealized hostile aspects of our relationship would be deeply resisted at this phase, abruptly popping up and then quickly pushed down again. An idealized affinity with me was important to establish before the intensity of his rage and sadness would be allowed to emerge. That is merely to say, this is how this unique situation unfolded.

And how did this occur in the rest of his life? As Karen Horney understood, the repetition compulsion achieves its enduring quality precisely because external events confirm the internal expectations. Projection works most efficiently as a defense if it succeeds in actually transforming the external world in keeping with the projection itself (and hence the mechanism of projective identification). At this magical moment, projection is no longer merely projection, it is fact. This circular reinforcement of internal expectations with external proof affirms the world view over and over again: One becomes fastened within one's projections. Character then is not only a fixed way of interacting but also a means of creating and recreating the world in perpetually fresh confirmation of one's fears and hopes. It is a way, moreover, of feeling grounded within one's solipsism.

Denial and resistance to change take on new meaning. Denial, by definition the failure to apperceive external reality, is a problematic term given the relativity of reality (that is, who is to be the arbiter of "reality"? As clinicians we can only offer possibilities.). External reality confirms internal reality which creates it, and vice versa; they are mutually reinforcing. Change (of symptom, of character . . .) is tantamount to changing one's reality; resistance to change is resistance to dropping what one believes in. To be sure, when patients change too quickly there is reason for alarm: Are we overwhelming them? Are they being compliant? Do they adhere to their own center or are we now one more in a series of lifelong capitulations to the other? What happens then when one world view is forced to encounter another? That is, how does the empathic enterprise itself impinge on world view and individual realities?

World Views Colliding

Empathic attempts are, of course, not necessarily therapeutic. A person second guesses (correctly/incorrectly) what the perspectives, values, needs of the therapist are, and then may acquiesce, hide, avoid, or struggle accordingly. As I struggle to empathize with you, you empathize with my attempts to empathize; that is, you consider my point of view, whether to help or hinder me, consciously or not. It is only to be expected that the other may fear such an intrusion—hiding is unexceptional. Much of paranoia (and transference) is a fearful and abortive attempt to mind-read the other's point of view, often with the minutest of clues serving to confirm a hunch, wish, or suspicion (Sullivan, 1954; Margulies and Havens, 1981). The goal is safety and self-protection, and this is why paranoia itself is churned by the confrontation inherent in asking questions (Havens, 1976).

Less evident are the more mundane capitulations of the self to the other, which can appear as a kind of politeness or tact. The stakes, though, may involve the risk of losing oneself to the other, a problem of centering or de-centering.

CASE EXAMPLE: BEING GOOD

Let me share an example from the day after I wrote the above.

A woman is talking about her feeling inadequate to her job. Though she has been warmly received, she feels that she won't match up to others' expectations. Now she turns to her fears that she'll let me down as well. "I'm afraid you'll get fed up. Sometimes you say things and it doesn't click until three hours later. Sometimes not at all. Sometimes I obsess about what you say, 'Why did he say that?' I wonder why. 'What must he be thinking?' It seems a little paranoid. I don't want to be a disappointment. It's like, OK, I'll be the good patient."

"So you try to read my mind," I reply. (Too harshly said? I immediately wonder to myself if she has heard this comment as critical.)

"Yeah. I do that. I wish I could stop." (Her response is in keeping; she is trying to be a good patient by telling me of not wanting to read my mind. Ironically, in her efforts to please me she is once again attempting to read my mind.) "I wish it didn't matter."

"That you didn't have to please me."

"Yeah." She associates to a relationship that felt very important to her and very frustrating. She had tried so hard to please: "What is it he wants? . . . I sort of lose my sense of self."

"With me too, you want to be the kind of self you imagine I would want."

"Yes, but I can never figure it out. It's absurd; it doesn't help."

"But," I continue, "you must have clues about what I want—or you would try to divine clues."

"I like that, 'divine clues' (laughs). Oh, that certainly opens up a lot." And here she launches into her fantasies about what I would like her to be like. In essence, she attempts to derive empathically (that is, mind-read) my ideals for her or for any patient.

Being a good patient can, if not examined, lead to a grand misalliance (Langs, 1975); the patient, out of fear or love, successfully second guesses what the therapist needs to hear. This can occur on a subterranean level, and a certain amount of psychological work can even be accomplished with a sense of relief and gratification. But the deeper issue of the patient's soul, the need to hand over one's center, remains untouched. In its extreme forms we talk of folie à deux, the imposing of one world view on another. In its less severe manifestations we barely notice (Havens, 1986); it is a form of getting along.

PROTECTING ONESELF AND EMPATHIC FAILURES

If Queen Elizabeth or Frederick the Great or Ernest Hemingway were to read their biographies, they would exclaim, "Ah—my secret is

still safe!" But if Natasha Rostov were to read
War and Peace *she would cry out, as she*
covered her face with her hands, "How did he
know? How did he know?"
                                    —THORNTON WILDER[3]

There is no one who will willingly deliver up his
soul.
                                    —MARCEL PROUST

Self-protection is instinctive. Impasses to the empathizer are thrown into
the road; the person does not want to be empathized with—the very thought
of empathy, another sharing one's innermost secrets, can be intrusive and
threatening. Of course, this may be a consequence of not feeling empathized
with in more fundamental, preliminary ways. Sometimes such a stance is
global (for example, with some profoundly autistic people). More often it
occurs in pockets of an ongoing relationship, for example, not wanting the
therapist to know about a particular area of shame. Masturbation, for example, may feel shameful not only in itself but also for the unique and individual
contents of the accompanying fantasy; it feels as if one invented the act de
novo. That is to say, it is not the *act* itself, but the particular passion, the
sexual preoccupation, this aspect of "me" and my world view, that is shielded.
Paradoxically, then, resistance can be a consequence of not wanting to be
empathized with in a specific way. Of course, the technical issue for the
therapist then becomes to share *that* state of mind. As Kohut has written
(1977), not only can resistance be a consequence of not wanting a singular
thought or feeling in consciousness (that is, intrapsychically resisted), but it
can also be an aftermath of not feeling empathized with as a necessary
precondition to sharing. And so the empathic enterprise is interpersonally
resisted out of fear or shame.

Moreover, this particular shame may also be the person's most passionate
area of existence, the aspect of life in which he or she feels most truly alive. To
reveal means taking the risk of losing what makes life most liveable, a secret
passion. Secrecy and isolation are preferable.

A deeper fear then may be a concern about *incomplete empathy*, that is,
that empathy will be partial and fragmenting. That is, you will understand
only a part of me, and a part that I feel badly about. Moreover, I fear that you
will identify that part as truly me. If, for example, you really knew my
longings and how intensely I feel them, you would think me bad, perverse,
sick. Of course, this can be true (the therapist, most people, might indeed
think that), false (it is a projection of one's own judgment), true and false (yes,
the therapist might feel that, but it is also an omnipresent projection and
interpersonal creation for this person—the basis for a projective identification). . . . It may also be a consequence of the inability to empathize-with-

oneself (a concept I will return to in the next chapter), or, to be sure, a deep personal truth, that what the person has done, though understandable, is truly evil by any standards and must now be borne (for example, a patient who many years earlier murdered her child in a fit of drunken rage).

Moreover, empathy always remains fragmentary by virtue of focus — we can't keep everything in mind at once. Similarly, two therapists can both be empathic and yet get to different aspects of the same person. That is to say, empathy can be sectored to a particular aspect of the person; in fact, it always is. For example, empathy with a conflict can begin with one side of the conflict ("I hate him for hurting me"), then move to the other ("I love him no matter what he does"), then to the conflict itself ("What's troubling is to feel both ways at the same time," or stronger, "Who wouldn't feel troubled when the person you love the most hurts you the most!"). The empathy can move historically ("Father was the same way, too"), can be extended into the present ("Like all the men in your life"), and can look to the future ("No wonder you feel hopeless about ever finding someone to love").[4] Empathy can be "good enough" — but is never complete, which would amount to *being* the other person. And even then we are never in full knowledge of ourselves; our empathy-with-ourselves is never total.

The act of communicating, which is shot full of miscommunications or parataxic distortions, is implicitly a confrontation of world views. How can I help — or hinder — you from understanding me and my point of view? Do I really want you to know what I am thinking? If you really knew who I am and what I most value, am fearful of, want for myself, would you use it against my best interests? Would you take something away and leave me more bereft and alone?

THERAPEUTIC COLLISIONS

> For psychotherapy to be effective a close rapport is needed. . . . The rapport consists, after all, in a constant comparison of two opposing psychic realities. If for some reason these mutual impressions do not impinge on each other, the psychotherapeutic process remains ineffective, and no change is produced. Unless both doctor and patient become a problem to each other, no solution is found.
> —CARL JUNG (1965, p. 143; italics mine)

Much of my discussion on empathy can be recast in terms of individual world views confronting, assimilating, and accommodating to one another. It is easy to think of individuals across cultures as having differing world views. After all, customs, history, heritage, and particularly language separate us;

"exotic" and "foreign" capture different nuances of the experience. On a different scale, regions, cities, towns, neighborhoods, and families speak to finer subdivisions of social world views. We are separated in time, as well as space, from world views of the past — even from our very own. It comes as no surprise that there will be conflict and discord when cultures face, attempt to assimilate and/or accommodate, and too often, end in one engulfing the other. Empathy seems different, a gentle process, but, as I will explore, at its very core lies the confrontation of differing world views.

The growth of psychological structures through conflict is intrinsic to the work of Piaget, who used the language of "schema," "assimilation," and "accommodation" to explore cognitive maturation. How do we build on the foundation of previous cognitive structures (schema) and grow in understanding the universe? How can new schemata develop from old? Why are we not locked into our cognitive structures; how can they change? It is the very lack of fit of new data into these structuring internal cognitive schemata that forces the dialectic of assimilation of and simultaneous accommodation to that leads to new schemata. *Contradiction itself is the impetus for growth and change.*

Empathy is seldom seamless, nor should it be. It is the struggle toward empathy and understanding that creates discord and forces clarification and, sometimes, the creation of meaning. While confronting another's attempt to understand me, I confront myself. In stressing the therapist's burden in establishing empathy, I have only lightly touched on the patient's need to establish empathy with the therapist. To be understood one must, of course, help the other to understand. Even the most primitive of communications must take into account the presence of the other.[5]

In trying to assimilate the other's point of view through empathy, I must be actively accommodating my own point of view. The other must in turn *help* me to accommodate, so that I can understand his or her vantage point. To some degree, then, the other assimilates my point of view and my perplexity. Empathy becomes a complex dialectic of assimilation and accommodation on both our parts; we must be mutually empathic to one another's point of view. (Later, I will return to these ideas from the vantage points of empathy with oneself and the recursive-self loop.) By my very groping toward the reality of the other, I am indicating how he or she must slow down and be empathic with me and with my confusion — in general and in particular. As a consequence, it follows that empathy involves its own inherent interpretative properties, implicit and even unconscious ones.

Interpretation translates the experience of one world view into the explanatory system of another — and then offers it back.[6] The therapist tries to assimilate the "facts" of the patient's experience, presumably facts whose significance and meaning are obscured by the workings of the patient's unconscious and defensive structure, and then fills in these missing links of significance and explanation by interpretation. The therapist's understanding in this model is of a "higher" level (not necessarily truer); that is, the frame is stepped back from the immediate perspective to a more encompassing and explanatory one. Insight involves a paradigm shift, offering a new level of synthesis. In order to be mutative, true insight in traditional psychoanalytic theory requires strong associated affect and knits together elements of present, past, and the transference relationship.

In a broader sense, something very akin to interpretation falls out of the process of one world view (the *patient's*) trying to assimilate the perspective of the imperfect mirror of the other. That is, the fact that the empathizing other cannot precisely reflect one's inner world leads to an unsettling disjunction: "Why did you ask *that* question? Why is this (or that) important to you? Of all the things I've said, why do you choose to comment here—and not there? I don't understand why you are confused—it never occurred to me that what I am saying is not self-evident or that you would be confused in this way. *Can* you understand? Are you seeing something that I never saw before?"

It is unavoidable that the therapist's wonder, the therapist's trying to understand, leads by its nature to an interpretive process. What had hitherto been taken for granted by the patient is now questioned as not so obvious by the very curiosity of the therapist. A collision of world views occurs; basic and personal assumptions are thrown into relief as just that—assumptions. The attitude of wonder and not-knowing itself (that is, *simply* not knowing, the attitude of "Why is that so?" or "What must that feel like?") is implicitly confrontational of world view.

We can speak of a hierarchy of interpretive stances. In a more formal sense what I am referring to might be called a "proto-interpretation,"[7] a precursor to the full flowered insights that provide the therapist with such a sense of satisfaction. I am convinced, nevertheless, that enduring changes in world view seldom occur because of the well-timed, accurate remark—years later they are forgotten. What matters is the constant examination and reflection on personal experience through the relationship with another who is participating in that pursuit. It is the process of two disparate subjectivities grappling with one another, accommodating and assimilating simultaneously to their different perspectives. Insight is both a cleft and a fusion within a larger world view.

Moreover, not all of world view is articulated. Much is simply our medium: We live in it and through it—and without awareness. (Water is the only possibility for a fish, like the grand pre-relativity conception of light traveling in an ether that we do not experience directly.) The idea of world view itself already implies a self-consciousness, a certain paradoxical standing back from it. Cultural shifts that we have lived through impress this on us: Old movies liberal or scandalous in their day become passé, quaint, or even pernicious (for example, the now oppressively sexist movie, "Easy Rider"). For want of a better term, there is an "action" world view, unverbalized and given in experience. In the therapeutic dialogue the given-ness of my world view is thrown into relief; your very wonder at my experience creates in me a self-recursive awareness.

This awareness of my subjectivity in areas not previously recognized as subjective occurs in fits and starts, seldom in epiphanies. In reviewing detailed notes of cases, I am often impressed by the tides of change that occur. Verbal insight is only one element swept along in the current, often trailing along after other changes have already occurred. Shifts in world view, insight in the larger sense, can almost be graphed by the frequency of themes. Repetition compulsion is akin to a number of leitmotifs recurring in a grander orchestration. I now visualize (auditize?) these repetitive themes as waves with a gathering force and intensity, slowly building to peaks, intersecting with other wave-like themes, all composing a larger form. I think it is a consequence of our medical, healing language that we treat these leitmotifs as if they can be surgically removed or conceptually isolated from the person. Alterations in world view are coincident and synergistic of verbal insight; they are part of the same process and advance together.

World View as Unspoken Belief: How Is One to Live?

World views and their inscapes are often dominated by a single preoccupation. It can be a symptom, a grief, another person, a physical illness, hunger, sexuality, addiction, revenge, a past event, a quest for stimulation and novelty, or even an affect. The preoccupation itself becomes larger than life and forms the gravitational center of the person's universe. Everything attains relevance and meaning with respect to the preoccupation; nothing escapes its sway. As it becomes more ensconced, the entire world comes within its compass. Clinically, we use such terms as addiction, compulsion, obsession — diseases of the mind. But to the one who endures, it is the hub of existence.

Khantzian (1988) describes the chaotic inner state of the addicted person as destabilized, "empty." In parallel, the experience of the empathizer is frequently one of boredom. Few would want to stay with this shared experience. And herein lies a clue.

Ironically, boredom as a phenomenon is interesting: It is not quite empty and numb, but itchy, waiting and irritable. One hopes for something to happen; this present is without interest — one wants to put it in the past and to have a fresh, engaging present. We escape boredom, leaving it behind through the finding of something new; one searches.

The addicted person has a highly focused quest — the search may be urgent and painful, but it is not boring. The moment of satisfaction itself obliterates the past and future; one attempts to capture the eternal, pleasurable NOW removed in time and space. One clings to this fleeting present, and, unlike boredom, the *NOW* escapes *us*. The searching itself then becomes the compulsive urgent center—as the longed-for expansive/everlasting NOW slips away into the stifling/hopeless now. The only escape is in the presence of the addiction, staving off time, finding the NOW when nothing else exists. That is, one wants time decontextualized and removed from the inevitable flow of danger, boredom, chaos, or hopelessness, free of the future and escaping the past.

The varieties of addictions can be as immense as human ingenuity and suffering. We seem to have the capacity to transform most anything at hand to a personal craving for a center: ideologies and religion, biological drives (particularly sex and food), and pain itself (either physical or psychological). Often we make the other into our addiction, our personal religion or universe. I do not mean to imply that passion itself is pathological and an avoidance of ultimate concerns, but merely that intense experience, *precisely because it is so clear and focusing*, can easily be pressed into use as an organizing center.

Suffering, any compulsive activity, can absorb the ego's activity, the self's identity. I *become* my preoccupation: my craving, my hunger, my grief, my neurosis, my horniness, my thirst, my rage. It is the center of my existence for this moment and sometimes for my life. It organizes me, centers me, gives me purpose, absorbs my worry and pain. And it dominates me in my relationships to others, myself, my world. Though in its oceanic feeling it can harken back to the earliest preverbal gratifications (Freud, 1930), it assumes a larger existential significance in the present structuring of my life. It is like a black hole in the center of my universe—nothing escapes. My present becomes bearable, my past irrelevant, my future an abstraction. I attempt to center myself by obliterating time.

REPETITION COMPULSION AS RAISON D'ETRE: GROUND AND GROUNDLESSNESS

> *The most important task of a human being is to make up his mind—what's for him and what's not for him.*
>
> —ELVIN SEMRAD[8]
>
> *I had ceased now to feel mediocre, accidental, mortal.*
>
> —MARCEL PROUST[9]

Insight and therapeutic change create tremors in world view. What will replace what I have known before? How is one to live? One patient at a time of considerable turmoil and painful self-examination had a series of dreams in which the ground literally shook and trembled. We cannot live our lives so self-aware of our own authorship of world view and circumstance. Like Hume's chicken we anticipate the dawn of each new day as proof of the next; we inductively derive, anticipate, and create our own reliable grounding.

CASE EXAMPLE: AN ORGANIZING RAGE

A patient came into psychoanalysis after a helpful and lengthy psychotherapy had become stalemated. Specifically, the patient had greatly idealized his therapist and loved and emulated him. This feeling, though, made it virtually impossible to experience negative feelings, which were in abundance whenever he thought of his father. What made this more than a technical problem was the patient's profound bitterness in the rest of his life, a rancor that was expressed in frequent thoughts of suicide and self-destructive rages that led to seriously dangerous situations, like driving recklessly after drinking. His life was organized around his rage toward his hated father: If only father had been different, his own life, he felt, would have been much more serene and meaningful.

As the analysis progressed, he openly expressed his ambivalence toward me and his sense of my limitations in comparison to his previous therapist. I was much more like his father: inept, stupid, an asshole. Parallel to this prolonged and intense expression of hostility to me in the analysis were changes in his outside life. His serious drinking problem stopped. His life seemed calmer. Gradually, the other side of his ambivalence became evident, and his longings for closeness to me emerged. With some perplexity he now experienced a new dilemma.

"I get worried about what I'd do if I wasn't angry anymore. It keeps me going. It drives me. Without it I'll turn into a fat load." This quandary frightened him and absorbed his thoughts.

Half a year later and now very much worried, he commented: "I'm feeling very unstable these days. Sort of like I'm in an altered state. (With tears) It's almost like, I think I'm saying I'm scared (cries) — it's like it's too late to turn back, to continue to operate how I have all these years, because it's made me too unhappy. And yet I'm very afraid of what's happening. Like I don't like behaving the old way, and yet I don't have any new format to grab onto."

Anger provided a raison d'etre for this man; it was the organizing passion in life, his sense of who he was. Existentialists speak of groundlessness, the profoundly disturbing realization that one's usual mode of giving meaning to life has been, and always was, arbitrarily chosen, that it is a subjective choice that could have been otherwise. Kierkegaard called it the "dizziness of freedom"; Sartre, that one is "doomed to freedom." How, my patient asked himself, was he now to live his life? The ground beneath him no longer felt substantial. Clearly, his conflicted relationship with his father was not only a problem, but a solution — and not only a neurotic compromise formation, but an answer, in a sense, to his whole life, of how he was going to live and make sense out of a painful existence.

Interestingly, an unconscious metaphor to his problem of working-through emerged. He had throughout his treatment repeated dream images of buildings and construction. Some buildings were undergoing repair; some were being torn down for other buildings; some were new structures; some were renovated inside, some out. After he had moved psychologically from the concerns that had preoccupied him early on in the analysis, he dreamed of an entire city being built (perhaps with some of the same grandiosity that marked his estimation of his first therapist). This architectural metaphor, though, is apt for the meaning I am trying to capture. Working with a conflict or a grief, it seems to me, is not like fixing the plumbing of a building; it is more like the consideration of an elaborately coordinated architectural design — the harmony of the building demands that one aspect relate to another. It was as if he were building up and tearing down one potential solution after another, designing himself, his past, present, and future. Ultimately this man did find a different way to live, and though the blueprint contained elements familiar from his previous life, neither of us could have predicted his new design.

CASE EXAMPLE: THE FUTURE OF AN ILLUSION

> *Unless both doctor and patient become a*
> *problem to each other . . .*
> —CARL JUNG (1965, p. 143)

A very moral man, committed to his beliefs, had been in therapy for several years for a chronic, deep-seated depression. Highly idealistic, he was constantly disappointed and disillusioned with life and with those in authority. Often he seemed to be swimming against the tide of expediency when he felt a larger value was at stake. At considerable personal sacrifice he would adhere to what he felt was right even though he got little support from those he loved.

He had always seen his father and an older brother in idealized terms. They were formidable characters, highly successful in their legal careers and very committed to excellence — and he had followed them into the law. Early on in life he had become bitterly disillusioned with the Catholic church for its stand on masturbation and sexuality, feeling that it had caused needless guilt and suffering in himself and others. He felt astonished that his father never came to the same realization, that father too simplistically held to the teachings of the church. Who could he now trust? Who was he to turn to for guidance?

With shaking determination he had replaced the church and his father with his own tough sense of duty and rightness, his personal religion.

From the start I too was idealized in the treatment. Therapy proved helpful to him; his more acute experience of depression cleared and his life in general seemed happier and more along the lines of his own choosing. He got into business as his own boss, and, after many years of uncertainty and personal doubt as to his fitness to be a husband, he finally decided to marry the woman whom he admired and loved. Nevertheless, it nagged at me and this patient that the therapy seemed not to involve me deeply, that our relationship seemed superficial, even sterile. Though by external criteria I felt that this had been a successful treatment outcome, I nevertheless had been unable to effect a deep change. I felt remiss about my own detachment, sensing that I had never fully invested in his therapy, that it had merely happened. Despite the gradual improvement in the quality of his life, there were long periods of stalemate, plateau, and boredom for us both in the treatment. A number of times he asked about terminating—we had gone as far as he thought we could, and that was pretty good from his standpoint. This seemed wrong to me the first few times: Could he go further? We dully accepted that his more chronic sense of depression would probably always remain untouched.

The shift came abruptly and with intensity.

Around some vexing and overlong delays in insurance reimbursement, he began for the first time to feel disillusioned with me—I must not have filled out the forms correctly and on time. This became a preoccupation. He found himself angry and depressed for days on end, unable to sleep or to enjoy his life. From my elevated status I fell a very long way. The shallowness of our relationship was exceedingly painful to him: I simply could not have cared that much for this foul up to have happened. Certainly, I was not as competent as he had previously experienced me. Powerful new memories came to the surface. Though he had devoted much of his life to patterning himself after his father and brother, at critical times he had felt abandoned and bereft of their availability and guidance—painfully alone, lost, with no external or internal compass to guide him. In therapy this was a time of grieving for his father, for his brother, for his mother (who had never had the deep caring quality of his father), and for his image of me. It also was a time of grieving for himself: who he had been and who he now was—a man, he felt, with no real center, a man who turned to others to define himself or who religiously, compulsively, took on values to give himself a sense of definition.

Parallel to this period of the therapy he noticed with amazement that he had stopped calling himself names when things went awry. These self curses ("you asshole, you jerk . . . ") seemed part of a deeper sense of self hatred and inferiority, always in comparison to an idealized other who would not screw up the way he did. He had a new vitality about life with a sense of possibilities and of freedom. And here he made a poignant insight: He felt scared and uncertain.

"Holy Shit! What am I going to do with my life?" He had always used his father, brother, and recently, me to delineate himself, even if negatively as an inferior. Religion, father, mentors all defined his life, his belief systems. Could he live his life on his own? "I have to have faith that I can structure my own life." (I wondered at this time if the religious and scatological/obsessional descriptors of his experience would spontaneously change over time as he changed. Would everyday habitual expressions be replaced with a new personal slang, just as his self curses seemed to have dropped away? More to the point, would his language, his verbal experience of the world and himself, change with a change of inscape? From my extended listening vantage point, they did.)

At this time it seemed to both of us that something very tangible had happened: We seemed more in the room together. I no longer felt idealized to the point of abstraction, disembodied and floating. I was realer, multidimensional, both in the transference but also in my actions. I realized I now cared in a way that I had not before. There was a freeing-up for both of us as a consequence of some more basic freeing-up of his internal life — and my own.

This feeling of internal freeing-up is one of the crucial outcomes of a successful psychotherapy — we hear it all the time from people who feel good about their treatment experience — but how would you measure it on an outcome study? Would the researcher also find that the clinician's interactions seem freed-up as well? I mean this not only in the sense of Winnicott's freedom to play, but the freedom as well to speak the previously unspeakable. The freeing-up of possibilities also carries a heavy weight. Symptoms, at least, indicate a way to live toward the future: They give us a trajectory.

Had I neglected the insurance? Was this my internal protest at being an idealized non-entity? I did not consciously — it was a "real" foul-up on the insurance company's part — but I realized my own quiet feeling of guilt around this administrative hassle, sensing that somehow it embodied a concern about my impatience and aggression toward him. Not only was I distressed, but I also knew in my countertransference heart that I was glad about the event. This seemingly trivial incident was perhaps inevitable: We both needed an explosion to get us to a deeper level (see Havens' [1973] description of Minkowski's [1970] work). It was not consciously contrived (it could not have been for these effects) but was a consequence of accommodating-assimilating, of coming to grips with one another. I realize now that a more profound symbolic action on my part — one that was about to be enacted — was not the insurance form itself, but my giving up on his deeper progress. He had worn down my arguments to stay in therapy and knew that I would soon let him go, empty. He needed me to oppose this going — it meant I had hope for him to be different. The insurance forms simply personified my not caring.

These events marked an unexpected nodal point in the therapy, and the changes proved enduring, deep and gratifying to us both. In becoming a problem to one another, we had for the first time found one another.

Finding Oneself: The Unlived Lives

Most of the examples I have used are in the thick of clinical work and do not reflect fundamental orienting features of empathy that I regularly rely on. Ironically, it is often in the initial encounter or the brief consultation that these markers are most evident to me. In these moments there can be an exceptional clarity revealed at the instance before we shut down in the knowledge of one another or in mutual interpersonal shaping and misshaping (Margulies and Havens, 1981).

In the broadest sense these are existential issues: How does one create meaning? What is the driving passion, affect, goal, fear, love? How does this person project himself into time? How does he hope? How does he experience his past and his trajectory of life? What is unspeakable? What is the role of death in this particular existence? How does this person accept or deny her responsibility to herself, her relationship to her own freedom? What is the role of renunciation in her life, what has she sacrificed? It is beyond the scope of this work to explore these issues in depth; others — particularly Yalom (1980) in his altogether remarkable book, Havens, Becker, Semrad, Kohut, and of course, the existential philosophers — have provided us a growing framework. Here I will turn briefly to the role of finite time, to me the ultimate context.

Existential workers would ask the following: Is there an anxiety that is specific to adult life, that is not a consequence of regression or a derivative of early experience, that is not an expression of the ego's needing to manage unwanted drive impulses and the competing dictates of the id, ego, superego, and outside reality? Is there an anxiety of growth and awareness, an anxiety that we must accept, even strive for, to deepen our lives?

In terms of relative emphasis, the traditional psychoanalytic formula for anxiety is essentially: *Drives* lead to anxiety and anxiety leads to defense. As Irvin Yalom has pointed out (1980), existential work turns this around: *Awareness* leads to anxiety, which then leads to defense. Yalom is referring to the particular awareness of fundamental existential truths like death, the burden of personal freedom and its consequent responsibility, the fact of ultimate and irreducible human isolation, and the drive for meaning and transcendence.

Let me restate this in the language of defense: If the prototypic defense for psychoanalysis is repression, then the prototypic defense for existential work is denial (in its most formal definition as the denial of the perception of an external reality that is threatening; ironically this reality is the impossibly abstract idea of personal death [Becker, 1973]). For interpersonal work, the corresponding central defense would be projection, also a consequence of anxiety—but anxiety secondary to threats to interpersonal security and self-esteem.

Anxiety, then, for the existentialists is a consequence of the apperception of terrible and fundamental realities of human existence. Freud confronted humanity with its animal side: das Es—the It, the Id, the Beast. The existentialists turned this upside down: Our tragedy is that we are animals who are burdened by our awareness, that unlike other animals, we are doomed to consciousness.

Robert Frost, in one of his charming/bitter moments, wrote (from Yalom, 1980):

> Forgive, O Lord, my little jokes on Thee
> And I'll forgive Thy great big one on me.

We face the life we have not yet lived; we do not get a second chance, and we are ultimately responsible and alone with the anxiety of structuring meaning in a world that has no inherent meaning. "The horror of death," Norman Brown observed, "is the horror of dying with unlived lives in our bodies" (quoted in Yalom, 1980). This is the anxiety of the adult, who realizes that time is not infinite. It is an anxiety that cannot be expressed as merely the derivative of childhood fears—it is the anxiety and challenge of experience, mature reflection, and awareness. Milan Kundera (1988) captures this well:

> We are born one time only, we can never start a new life equipped with the experience we've gained from a previous one. We leave childhood without knowing what youth is, we marry without knowing what it is to be married, and even when we enter old age, we don't know what it is we're heading for: the old are innocent children of their old age. In that sense, man's world is the planet of inexperience.

More than the symptom one fears the thwarted life, that one will never inhabit the nascent inscape and grasp that unlived life still inside. We are always inexperienced with ourselves, pushed by time into new uncertainties for which we can never be fully prepared; we are forever catching up with ourselves. As a therapist, I cannot settle these things for another—each time we grope anew. Ultimately, each of us has to find ourselves in our own empathic and self-reflective spiral, the process of empathy with oneself.

CHAPTER 7

Empathy With Oneself

Is the self portrait the portrait of a mirror?
—PASCAL BONAFOUX (1985)

I t's an odd term, "empathy with oneself," emerging as it does without fanfare in clinical discussions. Sometimes, inappropriate to the task at hand, I will ask the user to explain what he or she was trying to get at. There is something there, a crack in our language. What can it mean, empathy with oneself—to feel into your own experience? And yet the term seems helpful, so I became a collector of its occurrences. In initial evaluations I have never heard it used to describe a psychological strength (though clearly it could be). A meaning in the negative can be vaguely discerned: There is a distancing or even a certain toughness with oneself, a lack of compassion with one's own difficult experiences, as in "she is not able to empathize with herself." Sometimes an intersystemic conflict is implied, a superego harshness that is noted in retrospect as the treatment progresses, as the person becomes better able to empathize with himself. Sometimes it symbolizes a therapeutic movement toward wholeness and integration, the self knitting its pieces together.

It is also a linguistic solution to enigma. There must be a whole family of such terms whose primary function is to manage paradox, to acknowledge, and then move on from some fundamental, mind-boggling problem that would only take us astray or leave us paralyzed in our tracks. Like professional slang, it allows us to get on with business. Reification has its uses.

This paradox of empathy with oneself is intertwined with yet another, that is, The Self, an organic evolving entity—a process—that, in order to study, we crystallize into a concrete thing. The self can be defined as that psychic structure that comes into being with the enigmatic process of self-reflection — that is, the self as simultaneously both subject and object. I will pursue that further in the next chapter; in this one I will be concerned with a particular feature of the paradoxical nature of the self, that is, how one finds oneself through the mirror of the other.[1]

Case Example: The Mirror of Tears

An astute woman is recounting the troubling events of her childhood when her father had been insensitive and psychologically abusive. She had been the most sane person in the family, the parentified child. During this narrative she becomes tearful. Though it seems as if it should be obvious, I am confused and ask her what she is experiencing at that moment.

"I suddenly had the thought that this must seem a very sad story *to you*." It is — she is here empathic to me and my experience. She had just imagined *what I, as listener, must have felt in hearing her story*. Interestingly, she was not sad for herself so much, but for me.

She then becomes even sadder, this time for the little girl she had just been talking about, the girl in the distantly recalled memory, the girl she once was. It still is not *herself-now* she is weeping for, but almost a generic girl, *how any girl would have felt* in those circumstances, an empathy for troubled children.

Then, quickly, her perspective shifts once again becoming even more specific to her split off experience: She cries now for *herself-then, as a little girl*. This empathy is curiously projected into the past, capturing who she was then, and sewing together the scraps of that distant time, what her mother, sister, grandmother had been like, her school and so on. It is empathy with her historical self.

Only a brief moment later, she grieves for *herself-now*, as an adult, experiencing her difficult childhood. This is how she feels about herself — but now, in the present, with me, in the moment.

In a rapid succession of events she had experienced a complex and vivid series of emotions, each with a slightly different context and nuance. She began with me and my imagined experience of her story (that is, she empathically imagined how I would empathically imagine her experience as a little girl). The narration itself became a vehicle to recapture her own distanced experience through another: I served mirror-like for her to see herself. She then empathized with what she would feel if she were a little girl going through the experience she had just narrated. That is, she first placed herself through imagination into her own lost experience, as if she were watching a movie about herself. It was only *then* that she captured it in memory—a memory that is different from any previous memories of the *same* events because now *she* has changed and hence the context of the memory in the remembering-self has changed. Lastly, she could place her present self into the experience as the one who had lived these events and was now recalling them. In each instance there is an important shift of perspective from inside the immediate frame to one of being the observer of a larger process. The self-observing-self evolved, shifted, and encompassed more of itself through the medium of the other (me as therapist) and the imagination of enlarging perspectives. I provided a new vantage point through my presence, my wish to understand, and her wish to help me understand what it is like for her now and then.

In my recounting this clinical vignette, the disjointed quality of the experience may seem odd or unusual. I am convinced that it is neither, that this is in fact common in psychotherapy, though I had not been sensitized to the complexity before.

With this example, I am stressing a drive toward growth, insight, and integration mediated through the very separateness of another, rather than the search for wholeness in the needed complementarity of the other (that is, the hunger for the other that aims to complete one's incomplete self through union with an ideal).[2] Words like "mirroring" come to mind. No doubt what I am talking about has to do with Kohutian considerations of selfobjects, but it is more: One finds—and loses—oneself through the other. In this instance, the mirror of the other is the catalyst for change and the medium of self-reflection; the mirroring creates the observing distance that is necessary for recapturing (or capturing) oneself. One goes outside of oneself to find oneself.[3]

The Self Gives Birth to Itself: Evolving World Views

Part of the reason our psychological work is never done and that we are forever working-through is a consequence of the passage of time itself. We are always passing into a new life stage that has its own specific issues, not previously fully anticipated. These phase-specific tasks, hopes, crises, hurdles, and inevitabilities achieve their full force only within the life stage itself, regardless of how precociously mature the person is. As a younger person I was mostly bemused, occasionally touched, by the idea of mid-life crisis; it is no longer so funny. Milan Kundera is right: We live on the Planet of Inexperience.

But there is another pressing reason that working-through has such a circular quality. That is, the self must accommodate to its new self; it must revise itself continuously. A painter described how she had been painting on top of her paintings, constantly reworking the canvases to assimilate new ideas. Sometimes the paintings had dozens of layers, the earlier works long since totally covered over, each subsequent painting taking its starting point from a former one.

But my analogy does not work (let me rework it, paint it over). In fact, it is not like some lost art treasures buried beneath layers that could be peeled off—the layers were never that distinct or finished to begin with. It is more like painting with colors that disappear after a few minutes: The most recent colors can only recall by their presence what went on before. Perhaps a better analogy would be music, given its intimate relationship with time: Each note establishes its moment in the present, recalls past notes, anticipates future ones, and slips into memory and the past. I could go on; my evolving metaphoric process itself will have to serve as a metaphor for the process of an evolving self.

CASE EXAMPLE: A TRANSFERENCE SHIFTS

Entering into therapy a patient raged about a bitter, hostile relationship with his father, feelings immediately reflected in his contempt for me. We learned over time that the urgency of his relationship with his father was, to a significant degree, a consequence of the early absence of his mother, a neglect that felt life threatening in its dimensions. Father was the only one there in a sustaining, if deficient, way. We embarked together on a very turbulent treatment course, including times when he became seriously suicidal around the threatened loss of the women in his life. All of this was in parallel with his deepening dependence on me and with his intense feelings of my lack of availability. My own experience as his therapist was that I was an Ur-parent, mother/father, provider, the one-who-takes-away.

Only much later and with a working-through of many maternal issues did he return in his sessions to his father. This time our father-experience was different; the frantic survival quality had lifted. The feel of our relationship was more that of a latency/adolescent boy with his father, tinged with all of the previous issues, but fundamentally different in its quality. This father in the transference and in his memories was now a different father for him; it was a new experience of fathers in general, an experience not possible before.

It was not only that he took a certain order "to get to the material." Therapists have long noted, for example, that some patients regress quickly in the transference, and then seem to work themselves out of it. Others seem to start at less regressed levels and slowly become more fluid in the transference over time. Still others may defensively shift among transferences to avoid the deepening feelings that would emerge if any single one was adhered to, recapitulating earlier object ties and maneuvers (Jacobs, 1986). I mean my emphasis to be different: With this patient each advance or shift in his internal life required a reworking of the rest of his psyche; a change of world view rippled throughout. It was as if a colored filter had been removed from his eyes, some colors never having been accessible to him before now came through.

My point: We are always reconstructing ourselves from the vantage point of our latest consolidation; the self is constantly rewriting itself. In struggling with this book, I found that each additional personal clarification of my ideas changed my previous, as well as subsequent, understandings. Not only do I find and create my precursors in others, I create and recreate myself as precursor to myself.[4]

Rather late in life a man comes to therapy feeling lost about his life's direction. Though highly technically trained and with impeccable credentials, he has never felt at home in his work. His personal life, too, is in a shambles, his marriage about to fall apart.

About a year into the therapy he comments on a movie he had just seen, "The Tin Drum," that left him with disturbing feelings and strong visual images. I ask him about the most vivid images and he describes a scene of the little boy's mother eating fish, "animal-like," as she was trying to induce an abortion. The scene still haunted him.

I wonder about the mother in the movie, a parent and caregiver, who was trying to get rid of, abort, a child: Did this resonate with his experience? No, he says, rather, in fact, he had felt sympathy for the mother, the pregnancy was the consequence of an affair with a Rumanian lover and she had always loved the boy in the movie. Details of the movie now tumble out: a horse's head filled with eels; the father trying to get the mother to eat eels; the boy hiding in an armoire as the parents argue; the lover sexually stimulating the mother to get her over her distress and sadness—and the little boy observing; the mother then compulsively and disgustingly eating the fish, animal-like, deadened herself and gradually dying. I, too, now recall the movie from my own viewing and the horrific scene of eels coming out of the horse's head, an image of decay mixed with phallic sexuality. I comment on that image and how the boy watched his mother deteriorate—was that a point of familiarity in his life?

He recalls the intense visual recollection of the ambulance coming to take his mother away, the last time he saw her. He cannot recall any feelings, just being four years old and with this memory like a film strip. The woman in the real movie looked like his mother with a similar hair color and the "same skull structure." His life, I knew, had changed dramatically after his mother had died; he had been farmed out to relatives who were not prepared for or interested in having a child.

I comment that, like the little boy, he too had felt lost and lonely growing up. He notes quizzically that someone else had once said this very thing to him—in fact, the therapist who had initially evaluated and referred him to me for psychotherapy. Nevertheless, as a boy he had not experienced these feelings as such. It is curious to him: He understands how another person hearing his story would make that observation, but he simply had not felt it. "When I think about it now, I should have screamed and hollered—but I never did." I ask why he didn't and he replies that there simply was no awareness of doing such a thing. Not that he felt it was prohibited; it just was not a part of consciousness, or even possibility. Nobody ever got angry around him; anger was not part of the language of his boyhood life, it was as if it were a foreign tongue. From my perspective he had been severely neglected after his mother had died, not physically abused, but ignored as irrelevant to the relatives entrusted with his care.

It was not until his adult life that he had become capable of feeling deeply angry, and this when his first wife left him. Then he had had a dawning awareness of the experience of rage, that he wanted to hurt her. His sharp pain at the time convinced him that he should seek help, and this had been a new thought for him.

Recently he had observed that for the first time in his life he had been snapping at people, feeling angry immediately rather than retrospectively. In particular he described an instance at work in which he felt that he had been treated shabbily, that the boss had been unjust. Injustice had been a clear part of his upbringing. His referring physician had commented to me that by history she had learned that he had been severely malnourished as a boy, found dazed in the streets. His foster parents had not adequately fed him or taken care of basic physical needs. This, too, he never spontaneously brought up with me: It was not harbored as an outrage to him but a simple, distant fact of his history.

The injustice feeling too was never before felt—as a boy, he said, he did not experience it. More to the point, I later understood, he could not feel it: not merely because it was repressed or defended against, but because the internal mechanism to structure the complex feeling was lacking. It was not part of his intrapsychic repertoire.

It was almost as if now, as an adult, he might go back and feel what he, as a child, could not directly experience. Then he had no way to gain access to the feelings; they remained unelaborated affects.[5] It was not that for him the memories and affects were first in consciousness and then repressed, or even that they were in unconscious but developed form, split off from consciousness. For this man these feelings and memories remained undeveloped, like a crowded and pale seedling that has never seen light.

Is one function of psychotherapy, then, to go back to do psychological work that could not be supported at an earlier time because of the lack of an internal framework? One can draw an analogy to an adult rereading influential childhood books: An older person comes back to the same book in a new context and with changed cognitive and psychological structures; the understanding must now be different. Moreover, the book itself has changed the reader with the first reading; the reader brings a new self, a self partly changed by the book, to the second reading. Memories — and hence memories involving the self — must also be reworked, assimilated anew, by the changing psychic structures. One cannot dip into the same river twice — even if it is one's very self.[6]

As one gets "healthier" (or sicker, or merely changes as individual world view changes) previous understandings, memories, and feelings must be revisited from these new vistas. This circular process of assimilation-of-the-new-by-the-old and accommodation-of-the-old-to-the-new has a dialectic inevitability: One is constantly assimilating and accommodating one's Self!

INTO THE PRESENT: THE SYNTHETIC MIRROR

The same patient tells of a wonderful movie he had seen recently — but inexplicably he felt the urge to leave. He has no understanding why, though he can relate generally to the tension and stress of the movie. It is the story of a young man in postwar Europe who is desperate for a job and ends up stealing a bicycle so that he can work. However, he is caught and all leads to disaster. My patient could not bear to watch this scene. He does not want to see the bicycle stolen. Though there were many facets to comment on, I later say something general, apparent, even trivial to me given my patient's recent life's events — that the movie parallels his present concerns about his livelihood and losing his job. He laughs with a start. He had not thought about this though he had just been talking about work and his boss, and he hits his hand against his forehead — it had eluded him! (There is, of course, more that later emerges: his own guilt about his inability to maintain a job, his feeling caught up in a web of circumstances and being misunderstood, his doing himself in at work as if he were naive about the consequences . . .)

What does this startled moment of recognition mean and how did it come about? The sequence is: (1) He empathizes with a character in a movie. (2) But he does not know why this would make him anxious. (3) I empathize with the same character (selectively, as related through his world view to me, since I have not seen the movie). (4) I translate to myself why I think this would make me anxious. (5) Then I empathize with his empathy for the same character and (6) particularly why it would make me anxious *if I were him*. (7) He now has insight (some) as to why he had suddenly felt anxious, that is, he is now more empathic with himself. In sum, I empathize with what I imagine is his empathic imagination with a character in a movie—and this leads to his moment of bringing into consciousness.

It is of special interest that the omniscient point of view was particularly unpleasant to him, that he knew what the character in the movie did not know. That is, as viewer he knew the inevitable. This too is the role that I as therapist was entrusted with: I was given the scattered pieces of the puzzle, all pieces of his consciousness, though without coherence. Clearly he knew and yet did not know what was right there before him; the synthetic position was resisted and, in idealized fashion, given over to me. My empathic presence provided the synthesis.[7]

EMPATHY WITH ONESELF THROUGH NARRATION

After several months' consideration of his job situation the same patient comes to the following conclusion: "From inside my skin, this is how it seems: I don't like the job, but it pays OK and allows me to have the money to do other things that I want to do. I could quit and go freelance, but I'd take a big cut in pay. I've decided I should stay with my job for now."

I am interested in his conclusion; I had been following events with him and had felt his frustration and dilemma. I wonder, though, about his choice of words, "from inside my skin." Was it in the nature of an argument to me, that is, that he was presenting his case to me out of some previously unspoken feeling that I was pushing him in one direction or another regarding his work—or even more subtly, that I had an unstated, but clear, preference? At the very least the statement "from inside my skin" invited me to consider an empathic point of view. I thought about my wishes for him and recalled how in my internal musings I had been fearful about his finding a comparable job after his going so long without financial security. How did this relate to his having grown up under great deprivation emotionally, but also physically, that he had never found (allowed?) steady employment as an adult? Moreover, on the other side, I had often felt that it was simply too bad that our society was not set up to allow such a talented man to pursue his artistic concerns: to go out on his own might be truer to his gifts and abilities—but it would be hard. What a choice! But this phrase, "from inside my skin," had just been thrown in, almost in passing. What did it mean?

Initially, he did not comprehend my question. I explained that I did not understand his choice of words: I would assume that he would be presenting a perspective from inside his own skin; why did he feel the need to preface his point of view with that? He instantly recalls that he had had an image when he had said "from inside my skin"—that there was an outside-self, like a "casement or a mask with a face, a body, glasses, mustache, and so on," and then "there was me inside all of that." I immediately think of Winnicott's "true self" and "false self" and Laing's "divided self." But this turns out to be not quite right.

I ask him to explain further and he replies, "Well, I also thought that, from your perspective, what I had been saying about the job must not be clear, that what I was saying would seem fractured." In other words, he elaborates, he had been considering so many different aspects of his job situation that it must seem fragmented to me, too broken up to be coherent. He then has another image.

"It seems like this to me" and he shows me both hands touching at the palms and with his fingers splayed out like the letter "V." This was a limited perspective, and he had many of them. But when he said, "from inside my skin," it was more like this: and he made a large V with both arms. The base of the V now had himself ("me") at its center and encompassed the numerous little V's. For him the statement, "from inside my skin," represented a "transcendent" moment of integration of his various points of view. (This is not to say "better" psychotherapeutically: It could of course be a defensive resignation, a retreat, to deal with his anxiety of making a choice.)

In exploring all of his fantasies, hopes, fears, and thwarted ambitions over the months it was as if he had developed them in pieces and had been left feeling fractured. He had found little bits of himself, but he lacked a larger, coherent feel for who he was. In a sense he was now identifying with his ego, the beleaguered executive who now had to make a pragmatic decision. I comment on this, "When you say 'from inside my skin' you also mean a view that seems more despairing and depressing, but one that you feel is more 'realistic.'" He says that this is true, but that he also felt some happiness in his sense of security and in the decision.

His search, it seemed to me, was for an experiencing, integrating center. In this instance he felt himself to be his ego (without using those words). We translate the term as "ego," but Freud, of course, wrote it as "Ich," or "I." In Freud's metaphor of horse-id and rider-ego, most people, I would imagine, more readily identify with the anxious rider than the beast. The "I" represents a push for mastery and integration. In other words, to our western frame of mind, we often experience ourselves as being synonymous with the executive function.

Interestingly, my patient formulated his self in part through his imagination of *my perception of him*: I would see him as "fractured," this is how he must have presented himself to me given my perspective from "*outside* his skin." In trying to wrestle with my imagined perspective he is forced to redefine his own. Who is he really, not only outside but inside and to himself? Does he have a center?

The "true self" does not yet exist, but is constantly coming into being, changing, evolving—and sometimes retreating and fragmenting. In writing this, I note with interest my use of gerunds — nouns made of verbs — not *objects* per se, but crystallized *processes* (I develop these ideas more fully in the next chapter). My patient and I have not now "discovered" his true self, even though we both may feel we have arrived at something more secure and coherent. Not simply a thing there and behind a façade, the self is a process waiting to emerge.

Narration Gone Awry — The Personal Myth Believed

Sullivan emphasized that the self comes into being in its interpersonal matrix — even to itself (e.g., 1953b, 1954). Karen Horney (1939, 1945), too, clarified the interpersonal threat to the self, the loss of center to the other through neurotic mechanisms that ensure their own confirmation and perpetuation. Others have stressed the narrative self, the self as story (Sherwood, 1969; Spence, 1982), and even the "Personal Myth" (Kris, 1956). Such personal, often unconscious, narrative efforts are not only a matter of psychological integration, health, and growth, but also a search for subjective wholeness and the presentation of *interpersonal* coherence so as to reduce conflictual elements (even if the listener is imaginary or one is talking to oneself). Clearly, the self can revise its notion of itself for reasons not in Sartrean good faith, but to deceive others or to deceive oneself, to revise an image. This is not unlike how some countries revise their historical textbooks from time to time and even come to believe their new mythology.

CASE EXAMPLE: THE ACTOR GETS LOST IN THE ROLE

Initial interviews in clinical work are moments of exceptional interpersonal complexity (Margulies and Havens, 1981). Things are so open; meanings are so unclear. Habit and stereotype have not yet entered with the full force that comes with familiarity; transference and countertransference, which are the antithesis of surprise, are still in their early stages. My own interest in the phenomenon of the initial interview was whetted by a strange event that occurred in my second year of residency.

In rotation we trainees evaluated patients as they presented to the busy walk-in clinic. On arriving the patients would fill in a data sheet of basic information, and so one Thursday I picked up the sheet of my assigned patient and went to the waiting room to introduce myself. Soon after the cursory introductions I surprised this stranger and myself by a smoothly off-handed, "Oh. I see you are an architect." Stammering, he acknowledged that this was true — but how did I know? — he had not put this down on the information sheet. I remarked that his stylized printing was characteristic of the profession, wondering all the while to myself why I was being so dramatic and intrusive, why I was playing at Sherlock Holmes. I soon gained an insight.

My patient told me that he had recently had marital difficulties and decided he must seek treatment. His wife had been having an affair and when they had been arguing he angrily taunted her with his own terrible secret: He was not who she thought him to be, he had been an impostor to her and to all of their friends. Over the decade of their life together he had fabricated a personal history of wealth and privilege. Schooling, background, lost riches, and vanished family were all untrue.

Only later in reflection did I realize how rapidly we, too, had gotten caught up in this central dynamic of masking and unmasking. Transference and countertransference had been immediate and powerful: I was shaping and being shaped instantly by the relationship (Margulies and Havens, 1981; Sandler, 1976). Later I mused on the almost subliminal response I had to our first meeting. When I returned to the data sheet, I noticed that he had filled out under occupation, "Harvard Graduate student." Unlike most patients, he was not more specific. That is, he invited a guess, and I quickly jumped in without even knowing why.

Among his many and complex reasons for now seeking help, perhaps the most troubling to him was that he noticed over the years an insidious difficulty in confusing his own self-fact from persona-fiction: He had begun to believe his own lies! His interpersonal deceptions were elaborately maintained, he was always "on." At times, though, he had to ponder about his personal history to get the facts straight for himself. He so identified with his fabricated role that it was becoming his self identity—almost a folie à deux with his own split-off persona, an actor taken over by his character.

This was at the heart of his entitlement: He felt terribly deprived as a boy, that he simply did not belong with his family. His present relationship with his mother was emblematic—she lived in a nursing home out west, her mind gone from a series of strokes. He had last seen her many years ago and it was not clear then whether she knew who he was (maybe, I thought, she had never really known). In his thoughts of seeing her again, he knew he would only be able to go through some ritualized motion of taking her outside in a wheelchair, that is, go through a piece of theater. She did not really exist anymore; she was a façade of a person. Sadly, he could not draw on a deeper sense of a mother from his childhood. Most of his gratification then had come from an imagined family. Not unlike many children, he fantasied that he had another, royal family, and that is how he presented himself as an adult, as part of a privileged, American aristocracy.

But now he was becoming his story, his script, to others. What is more, *to himself*, he was his script: He searched the other's experience of his "piece of theater" (a phrase he often used) to locate himself. It was the Narcissus story folded on itself: He looked to his reflection as real; he was a reflection of a reflection, a mirror painted and put up to itself.

Curiously, it was his now shameful secrets that grounded himself to himself. In a sense, this was the pathogenic secret as identity. As long as the cat and mouse game of masking and unmasking remained an actively worked on veneer, he knew who he was. Ironically, it was when he grew comfortable with his deception and no longer felt he had to protect it that he fell into danger of truly losing himself — and came for help.

With this case I have explored some difficulties of self-definition created in the interpersonal, that is, getting lost in one's façade. The self presented to the other becomes the Self, and even empathizing with oneself becomes deceptive. In the next section I will turn to dilemmas posed to a self reflecting on itself, when empathy with oneself became problematic and stymied.

Dilemmas: What Is Me/Not Me?

Empathy with oneself speaks to a synthetic process of mind, a push toward the integration of experience. This, broadly speaking, is a basis of most psychotherapeutic work. But what happens to experience that cannot be integrated by its very nature, when the person is thrust into insoluble dilemmas of self-definition?

The concepts of syntonic and dystonic graze what I mean here: that there are aspects of me that feel like me, but some that I disown and would like to remove (hence the disease model of mind). When symptoms are discrete, such notions are more tenable (for example, a phobia of horses). But those symptoms more on a continuum, as with "affective disorders," become problematic in and of themselves, as our divisions into pathology become operationalized in arbitrary, complex ways. When we add an interpersonal dimension to the definition (for example, "character pathology"), the problem of who defines "me" becomes ethical and legal as well. But for empathy with oneself, such distinctions reach to the heart of personal experience and the boundaries of "me."

I could choose many areas to explore here, but one seems particularly relevant in that it is so mundane, that is, the prescribing of psychoactive medications. There is something about "accepted therapeutic practice" that is both reassuring and unsettling. Knowing that a treatment is widely prescribed gives a certain historical safety in numbers; things seem worked out, side effects described and dealt with. But what about the subtle side effects for the soul, for the meaning that one attaches to experience altered by exogenous psychic molecules?

I do not mean this to be a position statement about medications or to contribute to the divisive sectarianism that characterizes our field and clouds the deeper issues. Problems in finding oneself have always presented in a myriad of forms and situations—but our technological age creates troubling new possibilities and dilemmas for the self-empathizing-self.

I have noticed among many patients who have recovered from a psychotic episode that they become gun-shy of their feelings. Often they seem bland and obsessional, hyper-alert to how they are doing and what others may think. Strong affect is feared as pathological; intensity of feeling or belief becomes ego-dystonic. And so the world is turned topsy-turvy; the self does not trust itself and guards against the emergence of madness. Therapy must now address the aftermath of the self viewing itself with shock, me-as-crazy. Will it ever be possible to permit once again the spontaneity of feelings, to reclaim the everyday nuttiness of fantasy and experience?

As clinicians we often operationalize disease concepts in terms of "target symptoms," mental status markers helpful in monitoring the course of an illness. In this fashion, for example, no longer is the prescriber of medications treating mania per se, but its objectifiable, measurable manifestations. Disease then becomes: sleep disturbance, euphoria, grandiosity . . . each a target along the way to health. Side by side with the clinician, the allied patient joins the watch for the advancing and retreating forces of illness, adjusting medications accordingly. Targets, alliances—martial metaphors seem natural in this war against disease. But an insidious process develops: The self becomes a pitched camp, inspecting and suspecting itself in a constant scrutiny of its internal borders. Now the enemy has infiltrated the interior of the psyche itself: I hunt myself down.[8]

CASE EXAMPLE: WHAT IS ME?

A young man came to psychotherapy for the treatment of a several months long depression following disappointments in a relationship. With great expectations he had followed his lover to San Francisco a year earlier, uprooting himself from his life and hoping to begin anew. Now it was over and he decided to return home, frustrated and defeated, to pick up the pieces of his life. He knew that he was having difficulty grieving and wanted to talk to a therapist.

Regarding his homosexuality, he felt this was right for him and not conflicted. This therapy was a first for him; there was no personal or family history of psychiatric illness. In listening to him tell his story I was impressed that he felt disappointed with his lover, even outraged, but that these affects were not so available to him. As I explored this observation with him, he began to talk about how he had squelched his resentment. His bitterness and fury gradually surfaced: How could his lover have done this to him?

Over the next few weeks and in parallel to his work in therapy he seemed lighter and talked of new interests and an awakened feeling for life. Retroflexed anger, anger-in and becoming depression: so far it seemed simple enough in this first approximation. My assumptions were then rudely challenged.

Initially though, I did not appreciate the qualitative change that had occurred in his mental status. He felt better and I felt pleased for him and about our work together. His improvement, though, seemed to take over with a life of its own. He began writing an article in his field, a new venture for him. It soon became a book. He had the energy and enthusiasm to open a small business unrelated to his profession. His social life was now booming — and was going nonstop, around the clock. He no longer was sleeping very much; his thoughts seemed speeded up to me. Finally his boss, after wheedling permission, called me to express her concern about his sudden change in character, his new aggressiveness, inappropriate anger, and high spirits. It dawned on me that he was now hypomanic.

I was thrown into a therapeutic confusion: Had I unwittingly been the precipitating agent of a first manic episode? I was convinced that I had: By history he had never before had such an episode and, though he had been depressed before he had seen me, his "improvement" into mania seemed to coincide exactly with the uncovering events of psychotherapy. (And though I could argue the other side, that such a single incident would never meet scientific criteria, I remained impressed by these events and their relationship to my pursuit of a deeply resisted affect.) Of course, I had seen many dramatic instances of mind-body interaction, but the power of my psychological intervention (an "anger-in" model) came to me with surprise. What did this all mean?

As his feeling good gathered more and more steam, his work and personal life began to suffer. Clinically, it became evident to me that though I felt psychotherapy had precipitated the manic episode, my patient was not now responding to my psychotherapeutic attempts to intervene. In order to avert a hospitalization, I strongly recommended medications. I was shifting midstream to a decidedly more biological point of view.

He very quickly responded to the lithium.

> *In the sky there is no distinction of east and*
> *west; people create distinctions out of their*
> *own minds and then believe them to be true.*
> —BUDDHA

Nowhere in psychiatry is the Cartesian mind-body dilemma so problematic for the Self than it is with hypomania. One's inalienable (now alienable) experience of happiness and well-being is called into question. The confusion of "what is me?" is compounded by the therapist's own confusion (or, to be sure, lack of confusion) about such important matters. Mixed messages are built in.

We often make "as if" assumptions for the sake of methodological clarity (Zetzel and Meissner, 1973). Freud (1890) did this as a matter of theoretical convenience. In a letter to Fliess he wrote:

> I have no inclination at all to keep the domain of the psychological floating as it were in the air without any organic foundation, but I have no knowledge beyond that conviction so I have to conduct myself *as if* I had only the psychological before me. [italics mine]

Psychopharmacologists must make "as if" assumptions, too. Sometimes we even believe our assumptions tenaciously as a matter of principle and commitment. Regarding this particular patient, I might have been able to shift perspectives intellectually and pragmatically — but my patient could not. Mine was a concerned, but relatively detached, confusion. (After all, it was not me, no matter how concerned. As the joke about ham and eggs goes: The chicken is interested, but the pig is committed.) My patient lived constantly with this doubt: What is me?

During the early phases of lithium treatment, he precipitously discontinued his medications — He felt OK, what were they doing to him anyway? Had he been really sick? — and became manic once again. As with many patients, it was only after another depression that he concluded that he should leave his medications alone for a while. There was enough stress and confusion.

For me too there was new uncertainty: I began to doubt my intuitive-empathic responses. These were not gross and obvious reactions on my part; I was used to treating manic-depressive illness in psychotherapy and with medications, but that made it all the more troublesome — in the past I had glossed over these difficulties. Now I was aware reflexively that my very attitude, my listening (and probing) posture and the assumptions behind how I was investigating data reflected a fundamental question: Who or what was I speaking to at a given moment? If my patient was terribly sad, was that "real" sadness mixed with despair — or was it his illness? What was an appropriate level of sadness before I intervened? Not that I felt so quick to take action, but I found that part of me would now listen diagnostically for signs of reassurance, sort of intuitive-syndromic listening (for example, he seems sad, but not depressed; his range of affect is broad, he gets pleasure from things he is talking about . . .). These questions are second nature for me in clinical work, asked and answered subliminally; usually I am barely aware that I am making these distinctions until something seems out of line. Auto mechanics know from the feel of a motor, its hum; their ears prick up to changes. And now, with my more active listening, my patient was anxiously listening to me listen to him.

And is this at the crux of it—that my confusion added to the difficult process of empathy with oneself and the use of the other? If I were confused in empathizing him, would he then not be confused in his empathizing with me empathizing with him?

Similarly, and more insidiously, I wondered about his excited and happy times—more insidiously because happiness is usually considered ego-syntonic, that is, "me." Depression, for most of us, is a symptom: We want to feel different and so inquiry into the difficulty seems a prelude to ridding oneself of something unwanted. But not so for happiness, energy, and a sense of well-being—these may be our finest moments, the self that we aspire to. Now something basic to self was being called into question by our shift in attitudes and assumptions, by the process itself of prescribing medications.

In retrospect (and pragmatic concerns aside), why not, as therapist, simply take a more phenomenological or experiential view? Why not merely explore the experience (perhaps in a similar fashion to the dream experience in Chapter 2)? But I could not, we could not—even if we had wanted to. This very doubt about the self was for him the experience of being manic-depressive *and* on medications. It was a superimposed state of experiencing himself that could not be avoided—for him it was a central, existential issue as to who he now was. Our psychodynamic world had become irrevocably more complicated with the introduction of psychopharmacology. The experience of introducing medications—even with the most careful and reasoned clinical explanations—raises profoundly the mind/body dilemma for the experiencing self. Certainly we can avoid the issue as unanswerable, but many of our patients will continue to live with this deep uncertainty as to who they really are.

Descartes found his epistemological bedrock in "I think, therefore I am." The ground slips from under us when we question such fundamentals. One horror of psychosis is the loss of ownership of experience (for example, "they" are making my body tingle this way). A "disease of affect," a "thought disorder"—to what can the self anchor itself when the basics of feelings and experience are questioned? The question is not only "Who am I?" but "Is what I feel *really* me, or is it something that I wouldn't feel if my lithium level were higher?" Does the lithium get rid of some part of me-that's-really-me? It feels that way when it takes away my happiness, my "manic euphoria." But it doesn't feel that way when it gets rid of my depression, which seems not-me, alien. What of my experience do I trust as me? How can I even empathize with myself and what I feel when part of me may not, should not, even belong to me?

Surely for my patient there were other, related issues of identity. His homosexuality, though he felt it was his true orientation and not his reason for coming into therapy, was early on in his life such an issue. Moreover, in our society, it was something that was always there to be worked through interpersonally (Do I come out of the closet fully? Do I let this person know?). And of course there were complex feelings about me: could I truly understand him, did I care about him, would he do better with a gay therapist (that is, would sexual identity get in the way), was I like his father? These were critical issues in his therapy and can only artificially be suspended in my present discussion. I am focusing here on but one aspect of his identity issue that seemed fundamental to the mere existence of "biological" disease, the introduction of medications, and the implicit attribution of the causes of illness. There is no doubt that the intensity of the medication issues was overdetermined and fueled by other concerns — but still, what did these molecules added to his brain mean to his experience of self?

My patient and I continued in therapy for several years and this issue of brain pathology/self-identity, insoluble as it was, became submerged as a concern. This came home forcefully to me around the issue of continuing or stopping the lithium. My patient was blunt: The therapy had truly helped him through these difficult times, but how much of this help, this insight, had been integrated? Like a transplant, had it taken? Where did he begin and leave off? What was the medication doing *now*? I could, and did, give my most sophisticated understandings of these complex interactions. For my patient, though, this was not enough: The uncertainty was about his soul, and he had to know where he would be without the medications. Would he feel like himself? Would he be the same person? In a sense, he could not fully empathize with himself as long as the psychoactive drugs were present.

The medications were stopped, and we continued to meet in therapy for a while longer. He had no further major shifts in mood. Eventually, as with the medications, he needed to know if he could survive without me to define himself. And so, after working more on this issue, we agreed to stop (and as of several years post termination he had had no further manic or depressive episodes). Many manic-depressive patients are not so preoccupied with this problem of me/not-me. But for this patient it became a primary issue of his life.

Why, I later wondered, did I choose this case to report when there were other less complicated clinical situations that could make the same point? On reflection, I realized that for me there had been a special valence of confusion that I lived through in parallel with my patient, and this added to my empathic appreciation of his struggle with the forced redefinition of his self. Usually I arrive at a syndromic conclusion of manic-depressive illness on the basis of retrospective facts; either the patient presents me with this diagnosis (sometimes in error) or, in my learning more about the person, I recognize a syndrome that extends back into time. Most often this conclusion occurs very early on in the relationship; my diagnostic frame of mind is brought to the patient before I have lived much in the patient's shoes. In this sense, it dulls my empathic experience of the full initial surprise and confusion (sometimes relief) that accompanies a first-time psychiatric hospitalization or diagnosis, experience that drops the ground from under one's sense of self. I had temporarily ruled out manic-depressive illness (for example, no previous history of depressions or manic episodes, no family history of affective disorders or alcoholism). And so the appearance of mania came as a surprise to *me* given my understanding of this person. Indeed, initially I did not see what was right there before me. For a moment, then, I was thrown into an approximation of my patient's bewilderment about the ownership of his feelings and himself. We shared this experience: me having to rework my understanding, a shadow of his reworking of his conception of himself.

Philosophically, the phenomenon of empathy with oneself raises thorny, enigmatic problems. In the next chapter I will take up the idea of empathy with oneself in a larger theoretical context, that of the self and its inextricable relationship with paradox. This, too, is borne of necessity: these are fundamental human concerns — how we conceptualize ourselves and others — and they are intertwined with what we mean by empathy and human contact.

CHAPTER 8

Paradox and Possibility

*What an abyss of uncertain-
ty, whenever the mind feels
overtaken by itself; when it,
the seeker, is at the same
time the dark region through
which it must go seeking . . .*
— MARCEL PROUST

T he idea of world view presupposes a self; an inscape must have an
observer, a participant, a creator — a self that gives birth to the world it
lives in, that is, a self that constantly creates itself. The self then becomes a
converging problem to the study of empathy; each concept becomes the
back door to the other.

In a simultaneously written book, I would examine along with empathy a
parallel concept of self. This project would be in the fashion of Piaget's
series of parallel books on the child: one looks at time exhaustively, then in
later publications turns to space, matter, causality. The reader keeps in mind
that the organizing principle in Piaget's work is the unfolding developmental
process, the epigenetic cycle, and that one could construct an integrative
table with time, space, matter on the horizontal top axis, correlating the
developmental stages on the vertical axis. This would be similar to Germanic
timetables of history linking years with developments in literature, politics,
music, and so on. In this companion book I would begin with classical
conceptions of the self, then philosophical speculations, and later move to
psychological writers like Freud, Jung, Binswanger, Sullivan, Horney, Rogers, Kohut, Lacan. . . . To put matters into perspective, I would also need

to look at things cross-culturally (and perhaps even need to repeat the entire process from a historical vantage point within different cultures). I would particularly need to pay attention to those cultures that find the notion of a "self" altogether western and absurd. The mind/self conceptualizations of neurobiology and artificial intelligence would have an important place — they give rise to their own new language and hence to new thoughts. I will excerpt below some of the text of that imagined reference companion (and, for now, forestall the actual writing — the reader will understand).

Some Common Working Assumptions:
- That there is a self with which we empathize
- That we often find a true self behind a false self
- That the self is then revealed in treatment
- That this self is unified

Some Inevitable Questions:
- How is it that two empathizers can empathize differently?
- What is the import for empathy of an unconscious? (That is, what does it mean to be empathic with something the other denies or is unaware is there?)
- What do we mean by a divided consciousness (for example, "observing ego") and what are the consequences for empathy?
- What happens if there are many selves within the same self?
- Are there higher and lower hierarchical levels of empathic awareness?
- Is empathy synthetic through its very process?
- And what happens to empathy when the self doesn't behave as a thing (that is, a noun)?
- Can empathy bring a self into being, a self that heretofore was only potential? Can empathy create the self that it discovers?

Empathy has complexity and simplicity that are beyond words. The conceptual convolutions derive not only from the intricate process itself but from our tangled descriptions and definitions as well. Worse, minute *verbal* depictions interrupt the natural flow; our words get in the way and create new problems peculiar to language as a way of knowing. And because words become our medium of understanding, language mysteries are doubly hidden and confound our investigations further. Where, then, is the essence of the mystery — in the thing itself (the nature of mind, the interpersonal, the soul), our approximating concepts (they are inadequate), or our concretizing language (the words are obfuscating)?

I have so far approached the problem of empathy sideways. In searching for the other I am trying to live for a moment in his or her shoes. What would the world be like, out there in front of (or behind) me/her/him? What is my experience of his/her/my body, time, space, color . . . ? One assumption is that experience and world view are so closely intertwined with self that to know one is to know the other. Willy-nilly, in this fashion the self becomes operationalized as dimensions of world view. Am I saying the self *is* one's world view? I can't mean that, really. And now I am into a Wittgenstein language knot: this tangle challenges my understanding of what I do mean — and winds to a more complex web.

The Unconscious and Unacknowledged

Elvin Semrad was a marvel at going to the heart of the matter, particularly those things buried away in the psyche, locked deeply in one's soul. He explored the psychology of denial, and his treatment approach followed suit: The first stage of therapy was acknowledgment of unbearable affects, those feelings that could not be tolerated in consciousness. The second step was bearing and holding in consciousness what might otherwise be eroded away by the active repressing forces of the mind. Semrad moved boldly beneath the surface of awareness to the unbearable, the unspeakable.

A colleague once commented to me that he often had the sense that Semrad knew him better than he knew himself. This was my experience too in Semrad's powerful presence. But what can this mean: Someone knows me better than I know myself? For me, the feeling of being empathized with by Semrad (as a student, one could expect to have "blind" spots elucidated) was that he moved into those aspects of myself that were not easily held in my consciousness, even secret — but doubly secret, a secret to myself. These were undeniably "me," I did not dispute that even to myself (well, maybe for a moment) — but a part of me that was troubling or painful and that only at that moment became attached to words. My point is not that this is good or bad therapeutic technique, but that empathy can reach to areas of the person that he is not fully aware of, that he is avoiding through an active unconscious. I might have the experience of clicking with the insight about me some time later; indeed, in one instance the clicking extended for years as I grew older, gained experience, and changed my perspectives.

This poses another paradox: What do we now mean by "feeling into" another's experience when the person himself might deny that he even had such an experience? We are no longer living in the felt experience of the other, though we may be closer to his *potential* experience than he can allow. *We have stepped into a possible self's shoes, a self that perhaps now (with us) can bear the unbearable, a self we know is there but squelched, cut off in misery or fear. It is as if that person almost exists — but not yet. We are beyond the person into a potential person.*

Sometimes our reaching beyond the person into his or her unconscious space is embraced and we feel our hunch is confirmed. At these moments the feel to patient and therapist is that something very true emerges, epiphany-like. And sometimes our reaching is rejected, denied as "not-me."[1]

The Discontinuous Self: A House Divided

In the case of a conflict, experiential states may alternate, one after the other. I have sometimes been astonished to witness a person's obvious and repeated experience of a conflict and to realize only with my commenting on the conflict per se ("You seem to be in conflict") that he or she has been entirely unaware of the *idea* of conflict itself, that is, that he might have two opposing sets of feelings simultaneously. Previously, he had only been buffeted about by the competing forces, unaware, shifting from one state to another. This, of course, poses a dilemma for the empathizer: Where does one land in the empathic dialogue?

One existential approach is to focus only on the state of mind in the here and now, that which is given and immediate (Havens, 1974). A parallel and powerful analytic approach (Schwaber, 1981, 1986) also emphasizes the subtle affective shifts *in the present, in the relationship, now.* Such approaches seem to resolve the technical and theoretical issue of hidden states by focusing on the experience-near of the session. In this regard the experience-near focus has several points of rationale. One is to avoid imposing higher level theoretical constructs on the therapeutic situation. That is, even though one can never avoid the imposition of points of view and abstractions on the "purity" of the clinical material, one could nevertheless rank degrees of abstraction of theoretical assumptions (Waelder, 1962) and, in this sense, attempt to approximate asymptotically the "real." *This would be another way of restating the phenomenological ideal, the successive stripping away of the observer's layers of contribution to perception, revealing the hierarchy.*[2]

One can also attempt to designate the degree to which one's clinical approach more or less obscures what one is trying to observe cleanly. Without necessarily asserting that the "real" itself has any true form of absolute reality, one can assert that there is nevertheless a hierarchy, an ordering, to perception. Can I have it both ways (a language game)? One could, for example, examine the various effects of looking at a color illusion through a series of red filters, teasing out the contributions of each filter to the experience and ordering which made the most striking changes, all without assuming that "red" is an absolute feature of the object.

Another rationale, more from therapeutic than from observational exigencies, is that the experience-near will always seem more persuasive to both patient and therapist, and hence have a greater emotional impact. This is, after all, Freud's genius in making the transference central to analytic treatment — the most compelling data of all are right there, occurring between patient and therapist in the here-and-now. The transference may be a revised edition of an old play, but it is one in which both are actors and neither merely recalling in contemplation.

However, we are forced to make choices when confronted with some psychological states. For example, with mechanisms like splitting (and with the assumption of absent or undeveloped psychic structures), the empathizer's task becomes complex and paradoxical: Does one empathize with the presently experienced state, the alternate hidden (or unavailable or even not experienced) state, or the conflict itself?

It is interesting that my metaphoric language for splitting involves a different visual layering than that for unconscious. The unconscious seems below, repressed downward (see Freud's drawings [1923b, 1933] and consider his language, for example, "Über-ich"). With splitting it is as if the ego, or center of consciousness itself, is divided side-by-side (for example, see Kohut's graphs [1971, 1977]). What does it mean to empathize with unconscious material or "unconscious affects"? It is as if we are extending experience downward into the hidden. With splitting, it is as if we are joining centers of consciousness or even moving above to higher levels of integration or encircling larger domains. How does this all relate to the experiential level and empathy?

Moreover, what is the experience of "deficit" states? Here we grope about in our language: "emptiness," "fusion," "annihilation," "ego dissolution." What does this mean for the process of empathy? That is, how does one feel into a state of mind that essentially involves a lack, an absence, a fault line? I will be arguing that one feels not only into a state of mind, but into a *possibility of a state of mind*.

Therapists sometimes approximate this idea when they talk of being an auxiliary ego to the patient or helping the patient bear affects, thereby stressing the importance of selfobjects and implying that the very sharing of an affect can diminish its intensity. This is to say, the mind of another can be entered, shared, even bolstered in its precarious struggle with feelings. I submit that these lend-lease auxiliary functions do two things: One is support in the manner of a temporary scaffolding (hence, "supportive" psychotherapy). But the scaffolding also creates the possibility for new structures — this is, in part, what Kohut refers to as transmuting internalizations. The internalization of the therapist and the creating of structures begin only as possibilities. The scaffolding is the process of empathy itself.

Possibilities are what we reveal or even create; we feel into an aspect of the person that does not yet fully exist. Our patients follow us into that potential aspect of themselves: *They feel into our feeling into their possibilities for themselves.* (And this is why the therapist's own ideals, beliefs, values, thwarted lives, moral stance, and curtailment of possibilities — that is, countertransference in the broadest sense — need to be understood: We must avoid imposing our own limitations of imagination.)

See what has happened in the description of splitting (or self states, or unconscious affects . . .). At a given time we empathize with a state of mind (that is, if we are with the patient in the present, now). This state will of course not remain stable (as Sashin, 1981, puts it, it is "stably-unstable"). The person will switch into another state of mind at some point (state 2; there could be, of course, many more states). Our more distant point of view allows us to imagine the multiple states of experience, previous and possible, that are unavailable to the imagination of the other. This density of unawareness is itself an important aspect of experience and frequently contributes to despair and the feeling of hopeless entrapment — there is no way out in space or time — as when one is deeply depressed. If we were to be truly in the other's shoes we would be unaware of other states (for example, state 2), or dimly aware, or, if aware of the alternative state, unable to get to it in experience. Moreover, we would be unaware of a more integrative position (for example, state 3), a possibility not yet in existence. We are in the process of creating this other ground, working within a small änläge of the state, extending into it and developing it as we go, like the serendipity of a rivulet carving its own bed.

As empathic observers we are not only extending our experience of the inscape of the other (cf. Havens, 1978a, 1978b) but also taking the patient into an unrealized area of her own inscape, an aspect of her world view she could not tolerate before. *This new inscape, belonging to the patient, is paradoxically unfamiliar to the patient. We are into unknown areas of potential self.* Over time this area becomes stable, the stream-bed deepened, reinforcing its own meandering engraving. A change has occurred (an ego structure has been established, a series of transmuting internalizations solidified).

Semrad's straightforward language of the therapeutic process might here be reconsidered. The unconscious is kept unconscious because of the person's inability to stay with that part of self that feels intolerable and is split off. Perhaps, to restate, this aspect of self is not just split off, but is an unstable or inaccessible state of being. That is, *staying* with the intolerable was not heretofore possible.

Semrad's tripartite treatment strategy translates simply:

(1) Acknowledging: One enters the intolerable state of being.

(2) Bearing: One helps the patient stay in a previously inaccessible area or state of mind with the help of the auxiliary strength of the therapist's ego/self.

(3) Putting into perspective: The state of mind is held long enough to incorporate it into a changing world view, the river bed is carved. The bearing of intolerable affect creates the structure itself to bear affect, stabilizing the state of mind as a new area of accessibility (or structure).

Bewitched by Language

> Out of the slimy mud of words, out of the sleet and hail
> of verbal imprecisions,
> Approximate thoughts and feelings, words that have
> taken the place of thoughts and feelings
>
> —T. S. ELIOT

I return again to the potential of experience, that which is there and implied to perception, the "inner horizon." This time, though, I am gazing at my own reflection.

In the phenomenological literature "transcendence" implies the simultaneity of presence and absence-in-presence. That is, by nature of perspective one cannot embrace all perceptual aspects of an object simultaneously. And yet the object before us does not appear a façade; rather, we constitute our experience of a thing to give it texture, depth, and fullness of being. The feel of its otherness, its realness, is embodied in its having more dimensions than are immediately available to us, facets that come alive within the play of presence and absence-in-presence.

Similarly, when the self takes itself as its own object of contemplation, there is an absence-in-presence of itself to itself. The self of self-consciousness always involves the paradox of removing itself from the immediate: It steps away from itself and transcends itself in the very act of trying to capture itself.

The self then can never apprehend all of itself simultaneously. Consider the absence-in-presence of my personal past: I do not have to think of my entire past, to actively recall it now, to know that I have a past available to me, one that exists in richness and complexity. I never experience all of the facets of myself concurrently, but reflectively capture myself in pieces and yet feel myself to be whole. It is like trying to take a photograph of oneself in a mirror while looking through the view finder—not only is one's perspective limited to a particular and instantaneous view, but the wholeness of the self is obscured by the machinery of looking, by the impossible process of the enterprise itself. However, it is within this very paradox, this process of forcing to a new level of play of presence and absence-in-presence, that one *constitutes* self awareness. Paradox is a crucial, inextricable feature of self-consciousness.

And this is why one road to self-reflection passes through empathy with another who is empathizing with yourself. Though the goal of the empathizer is to secure an inside perspective, the very attempt to understand remains out of the frame — one cannot *be* the other, no matter how empathic. Empathy with oneself, then, can be facilitated through the decentering and reflecting medium of the other. It is as if you now ask the other to hold the camera and describe his view of your reflection. That is to say, you imagine yourself through another's experience.

The Self as Noun

> Doomed forever to conjecture, having chipped
> a few flecks from the lock that sealed the gate,
> we delighted in the glitter that gilded our
> fingertips. But of what was locked we know
> nothing.
> —STANISLAW LEM (1968)

One could argue that the self problem is only an apparent problem. In trying to define the self I am struggling with its many uses, both everyday and specialized. In this sense, I persist in transforming the self into a coherent thing so that I can then think about the concept in a linear, logical fashion. And here, because I am thinking about the self and worrying about its usages in a deeper way than I might ordinarily, I notice contradiction and paradox, as one usage context conflicts with another. As Wittgenstein put it, one gets "bewitched by language."

Our analogic models of the unfathomable create metaphorical solutions that are both heuristic and ultimately limiting: We now live in our models as if they were the real thing. We must continually build up and break down our understandings in our glancing approximations at truth. In the following accounts I will be drawing freely on different orientations. My descriptions are not meant to summarize the complexity of the positions, but to point to broadly different conceptual approaches.

NAMING THE SELF

It is useful to conceive of the self as a noun, a thing that we can name, a name that consolidates essences. I can now think about something that otherwise eludes me; I have packaged something evanescent.

How difficult it is for most people to use abstract, non-associative names, as in algebraic formulas or syllogisms. Names, a noun, give texture and substance — I can locate a name in experience, recall it, think about it. With naming, I go beyond the thing itself and link it to a larger contextual meaning. I wrap my package in the associative richness of language.

To name is to create. In the beginning there was the word — by naming, God created thingness out of nothingness. Havens (1984) refers to "performative speech," that by saying, I create. I pronounce you man and wife; if I'm a doctor, I can even pronounce you dead (obviously within certain parameters). As a psychiatrist, I can pronounce you insane, and now the burden is on you to prove otherwise. By declaring I create. And so it is with the Self.

Consider the naming of a child — what a responsibility! — we create the screen onto which the world will project. How difficult it was to find a name for my own children. Each name considered had its own associative burden. One otherwise perfectly acceptable name brought back the remembrance of someone unpleasant; another recalled a friend who met with unhappiness. My own name had been given in remembrance and in grief, and it had weighed on me as a boy, as if my karma was that of my dead, beloved uncle whom I had never known. I became the recipient of the unresolved grief, the loving memory. My fate was tied with his: I was a symbol.

For our first child, my wife and I had chosen two names, one for each gender. At the moment of my daughter's birth, her name became linked to her — she was real, a person, a daughter I had always wanted. Simultaneously, another person slipped into the shadows: Daniel, the name we had picked for the eventuality of a son, was gone at the same instant. I felt an odd sense of grief, as if I had somehow been expecting twins, one child for each of the fantasies that had crystallized around the names we had chosen. I realized that the very act of naming had created a persona in our minds, a fantasy of a person who was now not to be. Prior to existence, in a parallel possibility, there lived a self in the name we had chosen, a self attributed out of our own hopes, fears, and desires.

To name removes mystery. Is this why God's real name was not to be uttered by the Hebrews? It was as if God needed a name to become real, but simply knowing that the name was there was to be enough — the secret name, the unsaid name, embodied the power. In medicine we use the term idiopathic to deal with the unknown, and vexing riddles melt away. After a while this becomes shorthand for "accept it as the way it is" — and we do. By naming we stabilize chaos into a thing and can now move on from it.

One of Freud's great achievements was to name; we could now think about murky things in a rigorous way. Not that others weren't aware of the unconscious prior to Freud, but he named it and plumbed its meaning.

Similarly, Kohut rediscovered the self (at least, for psychoanalysis). How odd! What does that mean, to rediscover the self? — it was always there, but not in a technical sense. In order to introduce this existential dimension into psychoanalytic discourse, Kohut had to name it again, but now as a technical term. There is, however, a danger: Now we must fight not to lose it again, since its inherent mystery is lost in the very naming. To this end, Kohut (1977) wrote that the self could only be partially defined; that is, he left some aspects unnameable.

And is this then the essence of the need for a new translation of Freud? It is not just the scientism of the Strachey translation, but the fact that the radical mysteriousness of Freud was lost with our familiarity with the names. Bumping against the edges of language, our naming itself becomes problematic and paradoxical. By retranslating, we rename and rediscover.

THINGS OF THE MIND

A thing defines its space; reciprocally, space defines a thing. To draw something, for example, it is helpful to visualize the space around that thing, the ground rather than merely the figure. The aesthetic emphasis of the bonsai is in the definition of space.

Many of our ideas about the self come through seeing it as a thing in a space. After all, the very idea of an inscape is inextricably tied to this notion of inner space and inner things. Our predominant models of mind are spatial ones. Freud spoke of layers of the mind, like an onion; or "topographic," like rooms; or "structural," the Über-Ich, the "Above I"; or semipermeable membranes, one space separated from another with one way valves; or even horse and rider with its implied space in motion. Jung used the wheel, reminiscent of the mandala, to indicate polarities of mind and the potential for different colorings, as if blending from a palette.

Layers of mind and repressed memories seem like geologic strata, buried, not only in space, but in time. Freud compared the repressed and split-off contents of mind to the artifacts uncovered at Pompeii: they remained curiously protected from the eroding forces of nature as long as they were buried. Treatment exposes these intact psychic contents to the surface, to the light of insight; consciousness and ego would break them down.

For many of us, an intuitive understanding of the unconscious comes from the inevitable experience of loss and grieving. Loss implies another and unknown space — something or someone is gone, he or she is lost, and we are lost to one another. Grieving has its own space and structuring of time, and a grief model of the mind in psychotherapy has particular consequences for the empathizer. One goes back in time to a space, a series of spaces, in the inscape of the other, not unlike fossil beings caught in amber, crystallized (or, perhaps a better analogy, like a Vermeer painting or a Cartier-Bresson photograph, with time, light, and space caught in an instant and fixed permanently within its own universe).

> *Fair youth, beneath the trees, thou canst not leave*
> *Thy song, nor ever can those trees be bare*
> —KEATS, "ODE ON A GRECIAN URN"

I remember my mother, now gone 20 years, in the context of her times and of who I was then. Her memory exists in a unique space, and she is also caught in her own time warp: Her hair, her clothes, the political events of the day—all now exist in that time with its particular space and coloring, all through my eyes then and through my eyes now looking through those eyes then. How would she have changed over time, what would she now look like, how would she have responded to my children . . . ?

A grief, a life, is bound up in the particulars, in the past and in the present. Freud described this in "Mourning and Melancholia" (1917): that a person needs to decathect bit by bit and does so through the concreteness of things, memories, the stuff of the loved person. Semrad (personal communication) saw the essence of his approach as a process of grieving: buried memories and affect, lost in time and found in the details. These *things of the mind* contribute to our conception of the mind as spatialized, like rooms with objects, and are closely tied to the idea that the mind itself is a thing composed of these spaces and contents. Our theoretical language fosters this as well: For example, object relations, internalization, introjection. For the empathizer this is after all a natural consequence of living in another's inscape, with the uniqueness of that person's life.

THE SELF AND ITS SPACE, INNER AND OUTER CONTEXTS

And so I search the other's inscape, viewing the inscape side by side with him. But where is the self that experiences? I have concretized the screen of perceptions, but *that* is not the person. Like a rainbow, the self-that-observes recedes into the horizon as I try to approach it. I can only shift among models of understanding.

Jung appreciated the limitations of language: The self was more than the ego-homunculus of awareness, it was the center and sum of everything, the ultimate archetype. "I call this centre the 'self,' which should be understood as the totality of the psyche. The self is not only the centre, but also the whole circumference which embraces both conscious and the unconscious; it is the centre of this totality, just as the ego is the centre of consciousness" (1952, p. 115). The self confronts archetypes, parts of itself, that are split off and portrayed as characters in an internal play—the "Wise Man," the "Shadow," the "Trickster." This vivid language finds affinities to the metaphorical structure of psychoanalytic object relations theory.

In identifying the multiplicity of internalized objects, the object relations theorists forecast a complexity of self identities. It is as if the self that emerges is predicted by the constellation of stars orbiting in its object sky — now the bad mother is in ascendency and her sway is most felt. Our internalizations are like the gods, deciding our fate; one thinks of convergences and intersections. Like planetariums that project artificial stars onto their simulated, dome heaven, it is an externalized/internalized world. Sometimes voices emit from this "above-I" (superego), and if detached enough, they are hallucinations, disembodied. I do not know of clinical situations of hallucinations heard from below, as one might expect from the devil or hell's demons. Is this a consequence of early experience, with everyone bigger, higher, more powerful? My point is that our theoretical language and even the forms of our psychopathology reflect our spatialization of internal objects within our personal inscapes.

The interpersonalists, looking to the external world, find the self constellating itself in the social sphere — the context of the self is always within the interpersonal matrix. One could analogize to bees or other social organisms: The proper unit of study is not the individual insect, but the hive — no bee ever existed alone. However, unlike bees, we shift our social environment, and hence, there are a myriad of selves possible. Of course we mold the people around us, just as they mold us. It is just this reciprocal malleability that creates the self.

This brings to mind Winnicott's observation that there is no baby without a mother and predicts Kohutian selfobjects. Indeed, self and object are so intertwined that in a few short years self-object lost its hyphen for semantic precision and theoretical clarity. With selfobjects can we now speak of a self at all without being guilty of a gross simplification? And alongside these considerations we surely feel the pull of Horney and her emphasis on centeredness, the self on an elliptical orbit between the dual stars of its own internal center and that of the other. On one end of the spectrum is Deutsch's (1942) "As If" character, chameleon-like; on the other is the classical analytic, well adjusted, independent non-neurotic (now recognized as a theoretical, undesirable caricature). Gravitational pulls, centeredness, orbits — the self revolves around a sun of its own making or loses itself to another's.

Against all of this the existentialists stress our aloneness, our fleeing from our destiny, the creation of our own trajectory. Sartre's insistence that free will is fundamental to the human condition (that is, it is not derived logically, but exists as an a priori, whether we can bear it or not[3]) is perhaps the ultimate statement of self, ego, in its own space, necessary slave to neither intrapsychic unconscious (and with that, internal objects) or external social definition. Neurotic enmeshments and selfobject fantasies are in bad faith and can hide ultimate truths: We are alone and responsible to and for ourselves. In this formulation much of our self-preoccupation, personal and theoretical, is in the service of avoidance, of refusing to acknowledge our frightening uniqueness, freedom, and responsibility—we flee from the terrible concreteness of the self and its implications.

So where is the self? Is it within itself? Does it create its own larger space, like some cosmological theories of the expanding universe? Is its space defined from without, like a silhouette? . . . I am caught in a language game—I want the self to be a thing with its own space.

Ryle (1950) referred to the "ghost in the machine"—that the question is all wrong from the start, a problem we perpetuate through our language. He analogized the question of mind or self to asking the question, Where is the university? Is it the teachers, the grounds, the students . . . ? We look in vain for that thing because the concept is not inside or in a place: It is all of these things, and is simultaneously more than its parts; it is fundamentally of a different logical category. This is a problem of language, a "category-mistake," created by searching for the self *as if* it were a thing. I find intriguing parallels sprouting in neurobiology (for example, the modularity of the "Social Brain" of Gazzaniga, 1985) and even in the study of artificial minds (for example, Minsky's, 1985, "Society of Mind") with intelligence derived from "expert systems" which synergistically combine to create something more and which imply a theoretical machine that could think, have a self, and experience a center of its being. Almost by pragmatic necessity such ideas about the machinery of intelligence challenge our impulse to make the self into a privileged category that obeys its own mysterious laws.

Curiously, some analytic thinkers find such a preoccupation with the concept of the self a red herring, a theoretical construct that only appears to be validated and that is best understood in the language of personal and theoretical fantasy (Grossman, 1982). Does my cat seem to have a self? Certainly, and a distinctive one at that: He has a style, even a character (proud, sometimes needy, narcissistic, loving, with a strong need to be touched). Moreover, I know what makes him happy (turkey, scratching his ears, lying on my analytic couch): He is consistent. Does he *know* it? I doubt it. Grossman sees this kind of self as a fantasy, that this behavioral-self is a construct imposed on behavior from the outside, mistakenly inferred *as if* there were some inner structure. This line of reasoning is particularly ironic given the similar criticism of psychoanalytic constructs, like the unconscious, by the behaviorists.

In overview then, the self can be viewed broadly from the inside-out (e.g., the existentialists, Horney's notion of centeredness) or the outside-in (e.g.,

Sullivan and the interpersonalists); as a content of mind (the ego), as a supraordinate structure (e.g., Jung), as a narrative (e.g., Sherwood, Spence; see the previous chapter), as a personal myth (e.g., Ernst Kris), as a theoretical fantasy (e.g., Grossman), as a society of selves (e.g., Minsky), as a problem of language (e.g., Ryle, Wittgenstein). These are caricatures of subtle positions; I make these distinctions only to orient myself. I am up against language and want the self to hold still long enough so that I can examine it. Maybe rephrasing my language style will help.

To Selve: The Self as Verb

As the various theoretical positions regarding the self, even the theoretical non-positions (that is, the self as fiction), pile up in one's mind, the features blur. Borges once imagined a land of no nouns — the language of this exotic country used only adjectives (in a nearby culture, only verb forms). The expected syntax, the grammatical scaffolding of language, evaporated: "Nouns are formed by an accumulation of adjectives. One does not say 'moon'; one says 'airy-clear over dark-round' or 'orange-faint-of-sky' or some other accumulation" (1981, p. 114).

Understanding here is by connotation, meaning is a process (the words *understanding* and *meaning* themselves are gerunds, verbs used as nouns, processes that we treat as things). Understanding, in these lands, builds up by the accretion of nuance and association — like a drip castle of sand made from units without edges, slipping through your hand and taking on meaning only by merging into a whole. *It is all a context in the process of creating itself recursively.*

In focusing on the paradoxical features of the self, I find verb forms in many ways more amenable to those facets of self that present themselves in time and in empathy. Verbs capture the fluidity of the concept, its dialectical motion between people. And yet verbs are not enduring in my mind: I want the concreteness of nouns — an *it*, a *thing*, a *self* — something that exists in space. I turn to a verb that exerts its presence as a noun: all those elusive existential terms that express aliveness, nouns with a pulse.

Selving: Verb as Noun, the Gerund Self

Paradox has movement: The mind grapples with it, jumping back and forth with the contradiction, pulling away in frustration and confusion, coming back in hope. Maybe the word should be more actively put, "paradoxing" — it is alive.

Contemplating the self of the other in empathy becomes abstract in the contemplation, not in the living. The experience of empathy is in the encounter with the uniqueness of the the other, his or her distinctive style, life's trajectory, recollection of the past, projection into the future, and particular dilemma of existence. But we are not always, perhaps seldom, in empathy. Empathy is a process; it is there, then not there; it comes in with intensity, then recedes; it is caught, then lost. In my confusion I arrive at a gerund, a noun whose essence is that of a verb, a mental hybrid. We are dealing with "Be-ing"—the self is part thing, part process, changing, moving, cathecting-decathecting, never still.

I am told (by Dan Brown) that the Zen word for self is a participle, a word formed from a verb, and that there are many distinctions for this concept, the self notion being merely a pragmatic convention, serving the function of operating in the world. It is a social fiction—but it is not "real."

The Self-Recursive Self

> What an abyss of uncertainty, whenever the mind feels overtaken by itself; when it, the seeker, is at the same time the dark region through which it must go seeking and where all its equipment will avail it nothing. Seek? More than that: create. It is face to face with something which does not yet exist, to which it alone can give reality and substance, which it alone can bring into the light of day.
> —MARCEL PROUST

The self of self-awareness is continually coming into be-ing. It is that capacity of mind that constitutes itself in the very act of reflecting on itself. The self becomes itself in its recursive action; it is born in paradox and achieves its substance in the uniqueness of its personal, unrepeatable experience.

CASE EXAMPLE: THE BROKEN MIRROR—THE DEATH OF SELF-REFLECTION

Does the idea of a self-reflective spiral have validity in any everyday sense? Is this too abstract a definition?

Recently I observed a clinician interview a man with a progressive dementia. Initially, I was surprised by the affable and proud bearing of the patient; he looked so intact. The cognitive deficits, though, were devastating: He was profoundly disoriented to place and time, off by decades. His speech meandered to obscure memories, pleasantries, never coming back to its origins, aimless. Distant and early recollections, the last to go with dementia, were concrete and without richness; in the telling, his children and wife seemed like shadows.

The interviewer, demonstrating psychopathology to students, was very direct in his examination, and it was painful to watch. I winced at the apparent brutality of his questions — "Have you changed?" "Have you noticed your memory seems gone?" — accompanied by a running narrative to the students of the deficits being demonstrated. But the patient did not seem to experience it as I did through my empathic imagination. Except for the briefest moments of confusion at the questions, nothing endured for him. Tragically, he did not have the self-awareness to be upset.

The interviewer commented at the end of the interview that this man's personality was intact. Indeed, in a strange way it was, and this added to the horror of his situation. Even in his cognitive deterioration there was no doubt that this was a refined, gentle man with a warm style. One could pick up a basic underlying fabric of who this person must have been. But was his self intact?

For me, this was at the heart of his tragedy: We as observers knew what he could not know about his lost self. Only in brief spans could his conversation establish his self, like a mayfly whose total existence is compressed into a moment. He had no idea that he had deteriorated: His self-reflective spiral could not sustain itself; it made brief loops and died in flight.

A larger self, a self that would bridge time and memory — even if constructed and reconstructed memory, memory of memories, reflections on reflections — had crumbled and could not be rebuilt. He lived in disconnected time and space, reminiscing to give the evanescent present-self some substance. But memories too were now dying and stagnant, precisely because they could not be replenished by the present. A self-reflective quality is required to bring memories truly to life, to nourish and renew them, and to strengthen them within a vital context.

Similarly, he could sustain no deep affect — feeling was too fleeting to be elaborated. How he must have suffered early on when his self-reflective capacity had been intact enough to observe his own decay! But he was beyond that now. He could not even recollect the interviewer from the day before — his self came into being and disappeared before us. Not only could he not register new memories but, because there was no short-term continuity of experience, there could exist no ongoing self-reflective spiral to enrich and deepen emotion. "His personality is intact" can only mean that we as outside observers interact with deeply ingrained interpersonal qualities that persist. From our vantage point we construct his self continuity for him. Had we known a fuller personal history, it would have seemed even more terrible; as strangers we could hold on to a clinical detachment, observing.

Even in the interpersonal dialectic, the reflection bounced to the observer, but memory could not last long enough for the return trip to the self that empathized with the observer — empathy with oneself through the other could never be completed. The shifting series of perspectives in which one

finds oneself through the other could not be sustained without the backbone
of a self-renewing memory. Despite the dread in our eyes, his self sifted
through his fingers; he could not hold onto it, not even long enough to know
his self was disappearing even as he talked. He had lost the capacity to
imagine himself. His was a self locked within the moment, which is to say, a
self without access to itself, and dying.

Paradox and Wonder

> The creation of the world did not occur at the
> beginning of time, it occurs every day.
> —MARCEL PROUST

That the self emerges in its recursive loop is not only paradox, a puzzle to
be solved or put aside, but it is at the essence of the self. And so it is in the
heart of our work, hiding in its many reified forms of self-outside-of-self,
such as "observing ego," "working alliance," "insight," "ego-dystonic," word
symbols that serve us well in our workaday world — until we peer too closely
at them.

The reflexive spiral of the self is doubly paradoxical when it involves
another through empathy. The medium of empathy creates a supraordinate,
recursive structure that enables one to tolerate and knit together fragmented
aspects of the self. For the empathizer encountering an ambivalent other, for
example, an integrating level of empathy might be empathy with the state of
ambivalence itself, with the complex conflicted state of mind, rather than
with either simpler side of the ambivalence. And so there are parallel levels
of empathy corresponding to each level of awareness. In choosing to empathize with a supraordinate level of a conflict, I, as empathizer, may be
choosing a level not quite fully in existence: I am empathizing with a possibility of self. In other words, in projecting a self onto the other in the
interpersonal dialectic, I participate in the creation of a self that I now
empathize with. *In its very process empathy actualizes its object of contemplation.*

Empathy pushes the dialectical coil of self-reflection in motion through
the outer perspective that struggles to become inner. Telling one's narrative
to another helps one find and constitute oneself: The narrator lives vicari-
ously in the world of the listener as each tries to encounter the other's
perspective. The empathizer may give a more coherent viewpoint than the
person empathized with may experience, ironically because the empathizer
is removed from the frame and has a limited and incomplete view. Paradoxically, this may be clarifying and creative of the self at the same time. Empathy, in this respect, is a process which creates the self, either through the

other or through empathy with oneself. That is, the self defines itself through empathy.

In empathizing with one another in the spiraling interchange, we name experience and invent a new language in metaphor to crystallize that which is not yet either in consciousness or existence. Here we create something together, make a link between disparate parts of experience and synthesize in new ways things already and almost there, but never before there in *this* way.

It is fitting (inevitable?) that I should arrive here with a particular notion of self that is consistent with the emphasis I have taken from the start. I have been developing my ideas about empathy and the self in parallel, and wonder brings them together. In my focusing on the paradoxical features of self, I am really returning to the search for the other, that as therapist I can never settle the quest — nor should I. Paradox is wrapped in wonder, and the self is wrapped in them both.

Epilogue

Beyond Metaphor

*And at the end of all our
exploring
Will be to arrive where we
started
And know the place for the
first time.*

—T. S. ELIOT

C an there be an ending for such a book as this? I would like to rewrite
it; my present understandings are different from those I had when I
first started—and I am too. Will I agree with myself several years from now?
And will my perspective then be wiser, or just different? Borges (1981)
wrote:

> I remember Fragment 91 of Heraclitus: "You will not go down twice to the
> same river," I admire his dialectic skill, because the facility with which we accept
> the first meaning ("The river is different") clandestinely imposes the second one
> ("I am different") and gives us the illusion of having invented it. (p. 183)

At the end of Proust's journey in *Remembrance of Things Past*, he con-
templates his different selves, each in a different time, and the people in his
life now each with different selves to him, revealed in time and within the
context of his own self. And though Proust traced the vagaries and imper-
manence of Time, he seems to me anything but evanescent. Nevertheless, we
change.

A memory comes to mind, one that surprises me in both its abstraction
and concreteness.

My daughter, who was then four, wanted me to tell her a good-night story. She was excited and exhausted. It was late and I'd just come back from an out-of-town meeting. I was airport weary.

She wasn't clear why I had gone in the first place, though she was pleased with the doll and the Chicago T-shirt I'd brought home. Each day when I called long distance, she wanted to know when I would be back, why was I there anyhow? — she couldn't understand why I was away so long. My explanations over the phone became a kind of ritual each night that I called — but, now that I was back, how could I explain so that she would understand?

She picked the animals: I was to make up a story about bunny rabbits. And one, she said, had her very own name. We were playing, making up our own story world. By picking herself as a character (which was not always the case), she let me know that this bunny story was to be special.

"The daddy bunny," I said, "was going away for a few days, but he'd soon be back."

"Why was he going?"

"Oh, to look around, see some different carrot patches. Bunnies like carrots, you know."

She thought about this, it seemed plausible: "Oh, I bet I know what he brought back."

Carrots, I thought — but her answer was better:

"He brought home a carrot T-shirt!"

We had exchanged T-shirts, one real, one metaphoric, both ways of connecting to one another. The symbolic displacement worked in a way that straightforward explanations did not. The story was play, begun in fun and pleasure, part of a bedtime ritual of connecting and separating at the end of the day. For both of us, the story was a way of having our closure with one another. We enter a space, our own intimate space, created through our knowledge of one another, unique to us, painted together.

In creating, picking the elements, there is a mastery of the unknown. It is our story, our metaphor, our possibilities, we who draw the edges of the experience. As we were talking about the rabbits, I had wondered, at the edge-of-consciousness, on what level was the story registering — what constitutes insight? How much did a four-year-old have to know to *really* know?

My daughter, indeed, knew better than I; it was I who had underestimated her.

How explicit should metaphors be? Is the power of the metaphor in part a consequence of its indistinct edges? That is, to achieve its impact must the metaphor retain its surprise, its potential, its possibilities? (My initial impulse here was to say "shrouded in mystery" — and this makes my point: Reading that phrase, does the usual reader still experience a shroud? That metaphor, ironically, has died and been shrouded.) Part of a metaphor must remain elliptical, waiting to be discovered. Had it been merely a carrot that the father bunny had brought home, the symbol would have remained in the context of the story, and the story itself would have been rounded and self-contained. My daughter had given the symbolic bunnies a symbol once removed, affirming that my T-shirt was also a symbol. The T-shirt with a carrot reached outward, transcended the story, and connected it to the larger context: It was an interpretation of what we were now doing in our symbol making. Most importantly, it was done unselfconsciously—versus my own lumbering analysis.

And it was done in the space of play and caring; that is, the process of the symbol making itself was what was most important: Fathers tell four-year-old daughters night-time stories—and they delight each other. I was doubly delighted and surprised: Here was a new person. My daughter seemed changed, and we were both changing in relation to each other. I was away less than a week and things were different. And yet now I felt truly home again.

Notes

Chapter 1
The Uses of Wonder

[1]The term *epoché* is often used to describe this phase of phenomenological work.

[2]Though one may quarrel with whether "drawing on the right side of the brain" is really a metaphor for primary process or nonlinear thinking (that is, a metaphor for our more familiar metaphors) Edwards's book (1979) is nevertheless remarkably compelling in its approach to teaching drawing.

[3]Others have been inspired by Keats's relevance to psychotherapy. Meares (1983) explores the conflict of "technical neutrality" and empathy. Drawing on Keats's observations, he compares the attitudes of the "impersonal" psychotherapist and the "self-less" poet. His thesis, though different, is consistent with several of my own ideas. Stanley Leavy's paper on Keats (1970) is remarkable for its erudition and sweep.

[4]In appropriating Gerard Manley Hopkins's wonderful term "inscape," I have, no doubt, added my own emphasis and idiosyncratic meaning and drifted from his rather elaborate intent. Hopkins's use of the term indicated a divine essence or nature; my own use is more prosaic. MacKenzie (1981) summarizes Hopkins's term: "In [the] stricter sense, inscape is not a superficial appearance; rather it is the expression of the inner core of individuality, perceived in moments of insight by an onlooker who is in full harmony with the being he is observing. It is the distinctive character (almost a 'personality') given by the Creator to a particular species of

rock or tree or animal" (1981). The *Oxford English Dictionary* (Supplement, 1976) took up the term and defined it: "The individual or essential quality of a thing; the uniqueness of an observed object, scene, event, etc." The concern with essences is of course in the spirit of my use of inscape, though I am pressing the term into service to designate the subjective, *in*terior land*scape* (including, of course, the experience of others) that one lives in and constructs in a totally unique fashion: one's experience of the world, though felt as given, is always personalized. I am focusing not only on the uniqueness of another, but the uniqueness of the other's experience, a subjective point of view that the empathizer tries to enter (approximate) within his or her own unique inscape, the position of one person trying to comprehend the lived experience of another. Other terms, like "world view," would also approach the meaning here, but have their own freight of connotation.

Chapter 2
The Sensory Dimensions

[1]Any worker in this area must acknowledge a great debt to the pioneering investigations of Minkowski (1970), Binswanger (1944, 1975) and Straus (1948, 1966). Ellenberger (1958, 1970), too, has not only made the work of these psychological phenomenologists accessible but has beautifully surveyed and synthesized the complex literature of the field (1958, 1970).

[2]I would refer the reader to M. Robert Gardner's (1983) unusually fine rendering of the delicate, mutual evocation of associations, especially of visual image, in a clinical encounter.

[3]However, Daniel Stern (1985), Peter Wolff (1966a), and others have clarified just how organized much of infantile experience actually is — far less inchoate than our theories had indicated.

[4]The felicitous term *lived moment* I first heard used by Stern regarding explorations into the units of experience in child research (presentation, April, 1988, Psychoanalytic Institute of New England, East). His use of the word is with more precision than my own. Perhaps I am corrupting the phrase into common parlance.

Chapter 3
Pursuing the Unique

[1]In mathematics these reactions, appropriately enough, are best described by "catastrophe theory," a branch of topology that explores the effects of gradually changing variables that lead to sudden and discontinuous changes. In many ways this model is better for psychodynamic descriptions than are our usual simplified models of vectors. Sashin (1985) has ingeniously explored the implications for psychodynamic understandings.

[2]Havens (1962) has written on the spatial configurations of hallucinations in terms of internalization and externalization of objects and their relation to regression and healing over the course of an illness.

[3]The other side of this human assumption is the repulsion some feel with the Turing hypothesis about artificial intelligence, that is, the only true test for real intelligence is whether a machine/being can give convincing answers in a dialogue, without the observer having to appeal to the actual inner workings. We want to say, could a machine possibly have an internal life, an inscape, a soul? Here we are loathe to empathize, it is almost unimaginable — is nothing sacred? In an amusing and creative paper, Nagel (1974) raises the impossibility of empathy with another species, and in so doing explores the general problem of knowing another's mind.

[4]In his *Meditations*, Descartes did in fact explore the experience of pain as a metaphysical bedrock for existence (see Leder [1987]). I remember my daughter's first self conscious experience of physical pain, I mean the real experience of lingering pain that does not go away with a kiss. Despite our holding her, reassuring her, she had crossed a developmental threshold — a kiss

no longer took the pain away. "I feel alone," she said. This was heartbreaking to me, and part of my own development as a young parent; I would not be able to protect her from life's hurts. We could not take the pain away—it was hers alone, no matter that I would have traded places. She had to endure it: It was a self-defining event. This is mundane experience, but we both seemed older in the ways of the world.

[5]Morris Stambler, personal communication.

Chapter 4
Active Empathy

[1]Apart from empathy, of course, the notion of tragedy has included the sense of the inevitable, that we know by esthetic distance and by omniscient perspective what the character does not; we observe the personal flaw working itself out to its destiny.

[2]A number of investigators have explored just this use of manipulating fantasy and imagery toward therapeutic goals (see, for example, Mardi Horowitz's review, 1983). My goal here is empathic, that is to elaborate as fully as possible for me the inner felt experience of another. New images may, of course, appear as a consequence.

[3]It is fascinating to me that I find myself groping for the same words that the early depth psychologists had already used. "Complex," the association of memory traces, affects, and sensations, captures part of the idea here. It seems, in a more modern sense, that much of the alienation from self, narcissistic "splits" vertical and otherwise, are related concepts: the problem of fragmentation of experience and the psychic push for integration.

[4]"Edge-of-awareness" experience of the therapist is described poetically (the only true voice of such moments) in M. Robert Gardner's volume, *Self Inquiry* (1983).

[5]Schwaber (1984) says this eloquently:

> By our resonance of alikeness, we try to find our patient's experience, but in the doing, we must not confuse patient with us; we must know that his world is not our world, her psychic reality not ours. A patient's early losses may touch reverberations in me of my own early losses, by which, in turn, I can more fully hear the patient's; but my experience was not hers nor his, and must not be the mold for it. Thus, a paradox: it is our mutuality which allows us to discover our individuality; the more we find our echoes of alikeness, the more we enhance the possibility of locating our differences.

Chapter 5
An Extended Search

[1]See Howard Gardner (1985) on how observers presume a narrative form on situations. He cites Rumelhart's (1975) notion of a *"story grammar,* an underlying set of assumptions about how the plot of an ordinary story will unfold." Also see Spence's discussion of the pervasiveness of narrative imposition in clinical and everyday life (1982).

[2]Forgive me: Now I am in the position of trying to empathize with the reader's trying to empathize with my trying to empathize with the reader . . .

[3]I noticed a parallel phenomenon when I first began to take analytic process notes for training purposes. It had been years since I had taken such detailed notes; as a resident I found it intrusive during face-to-face sessions, and following Freud's advice (1912), abandoned it. Now, taking notes behind the couch, I noticed how my pronouns became confused in my notebook. For example, sometimes in my notes "me" meant me, but sometimes it meant the patient (that is, it was a quote, a paraphrase—but decidedly from the patient's vantage point). At the time I

resolved the logistical issue by always writing notes from the patient's vantage point: "me" meant the patient, "you" meant me. How curious this was! I felt like Keats with "no Identity . . . filling some other Body" (1958, p. 387).

4Ellenberger (1970) reviews this interesting literature in his remarkable book, *The Discovery of the Unconscious*. Carl Jung particularly took up the curative aspects of talking about such hidden areas.

Chapter 6
Reflections on World View

1The "bubble has burst" phenomenon is best described by "catastrophe theory." See Sashin (1985) and footnote to Chapter 3.

2In an interesting parallel to this metaphor, one patient who felt very stuck in his life, unable to move from an oppressive set of personal entanglements because of grief for the past and fear for his independence, had recurrent dreams in which he was driving in a car and unable to stop — there were no brakes or controls. In a panic, he kept safe by approximating stopping: He drove the car in circles. This too was symbolic of his feeling about his treatment.

3As quoted in Yalom (1980).

4See Havens discussions of the language of empathy, particularly the notion of "extensions" (1978b, 1986).

5And perhaps this is at the heart of the meaning of autism — the wish not to communicate, to be left alone, not to be assaulted by another's presence. To the other it is the absence of an expectable empathic reciprocity that feels so creepy, mechanical, and alien.

6The dictionary definition of interpret is to explain or bring out the meaning of something (*Webster's Unabridged Dictionary*, 2nd Ed). In their glossary of psychoanalytic terms Moore and Fine (1968) summarize: "We reconstruct events, but we interpret meanings." Meaning is by its very nature highly personal and subject to world view. One could argue that reconstruction is also an intepretation.

7Bennett Simon (personal communication) first suggested this term to me.

8As quoted in Rako and Mazer (1980, p. 76).

9From C. K. Scott Moncrieff's translation (1928) of Proust's *Remembrance of Things Past*. Kilmartin (1981) changes "accidental" to "contingent" — which captures the "thrownness" of experience: We feel thrown into our lives by fate, chance.

Chapter 7
Empathy With Oneself

1It often happens that one develops an idea first and then can later intelligently search the literature as one's own thoughts are more consolidated. Buie (1984) cites "empathy with himself" as an example of "imprecision in the use of the term 'empathy'. . . . Here empathy is confounded with introspection and is extended to encompass the additional meanings of perspective and sympathy in viewing one's self" (pp. 134–135). Kohut, though, obviously saw the term as helpful (for example, " . . . it is in the long run the task of the analysis to allow the analysand to become sufficiently empathic with himself . . . " [1977, p. 125]). Grotstein (1984) developed an idea parallel to my own in his emphasis on the self's relation to itself. He explores the "the abandonment of an empathic relationship toward the self by the self (the *I* rejects the self)" (p. 213) and its developmental roots in early empathic failures by parents.

The cognitive sciences, too, have a relevant literature: The whole notion of empathy with oneself is of course speaking to the concept of recursion, which I explore further in Chapter 8.

Bruner (1986) defines recursion as "the process whereby the mind or a computer program loops back on the output of a prior computation and treats it as a given that can be the input for the next operation." He further observes: "Any formal theory of mind is helpless without recursion, for without it it is impossible to account for thoughts on thoughts, thoughts on thoughts on thoughts, up to whatever level of abstraction is necessary." He particularly credits Johnson-Laird with the notion of "recursion to account for how the mind turns around on itself to create something like a sense of 'self'" (p. 97). Johnson-Laird (1983) explores how in principle "self-reflective automata" could act and communicate intentionally, think about themselves, and thereby meet the criteria for self-awareness.

2It is now taken for granted that such functions are critical to growth and integration, that normally selfobjects persist throughout a lifetime. Feminist contributions, too, have called into question single-minded focus on separation and individuation as being loaded with antique and masculine value judgements about what is proper adult and healthy relating (that is, women have always been more at ease with interdependency. See, for example, Gilligan, 1982).

3In art and literature we speak of aesthetic distance, the requisite emotional distance to capture experience. Analogously, in historical studies we need a distance in time: It is hard for us to explore ourselves in the present. Our selves need to change first, shift their perspectives — we need to be outside of ourselves, as it were — before we can locate ourselves. Oddly, the very proximity to experience can make it difficult to assimilate.

4Many have studied similar concepts with respect to memory, the idea of "memories of memories." See, for example, Freud's discussion in the Rat Man case (1909) of memories overdetermined and forever reworked, Peter Wolff's discussion of the real versus the recollected past (1966b), and even the literature of artificial intelligence (Minsky, 1987).

5Basch (1983) makes helpful distinctions here among affects, feelings, and emotions, each on an increasing level of psychological complexity and density of experience.

6Hofstadter (1979) makes a similar argument regarding a fundamental fallacy of anatomical neurophysiological reductionism: There can never be a simple point-to-point correspondence of anatomical description and "mind" (or even the same brain to itself or the same mind to the same mind — these are not "things" that ever stay still long enough!).

7And, if this remains unexamined over the course of his treatment, it could serve as a powerful resistance to his own synthesizing. That is, part of the work of treatment is to develop just this sense of empathy with oneself (similar to, for example, "identifying with the analyzing function" of the analyst).

8And, as John Mack emphasizes (personal communication), aren't affects at the center of our being? That is, aiming medications at affects that cannot be handled, treating them as target symptoms, we shoot at our own center.

Chapter 8
Paradox and Possibility

1Havens (1986) has suggested that one test of empathy is whether the empathizer can complete the other's sentence in his/her mind's ear. This would ironically imply that empathic validation in part might be external to the person's ability to confirm or not confirm.

2One could draw a parallel to the idea of the "hierarchy of defense mechanisms" (Semrad, 1973; Vaillant, 1976, 1977) — that "health" can be operationalized by the degree to which one's defenses sacrifice up reality to maintain a tolerable psychological state.

3Once again Yalom's (1980) work is remarkable for its sweep and intellectual accessibility. Hanly's (1979) illuminating discussion of Sartre is also helpful here.

Bibliography

Austin, J. L. (1962). *How To Do Things with Words*. Cambridge: Harvard University Press.

Baker, H. S. & Baker, M. N. (1987). Heinz Kohut's self psychology: An overview. *American Journal of Psychiatry*, 144:1–9.

Basch, M. F. (1983). Empathic understanding: A review of the concept and some theoretical considerations. *Journal of the American Psychoanalytic Association*, 31: 101–126.

Bate, W. J. (1964). *John Keats*. Cambridge: Harvard University Press.

Bate, W. J. (1982). An examination of imagination. *The New York Review of Books*, (November 18): 71–73.

Becker, E. (1973). *The Denial of Death*. New York: Macmillan.

Bibring, E. (1943). The conception of the repetition compulsion. *The Psychoanalytic Quarterly*, 12: 486–519.

Binswanger, L. (1944). The case of Ellen West. In R. May, E. Angel, & H. F. Ellenberger (Eds.), *Existence*. New York: Basic Books, 1958.

Binswanger, L. (1975). *Being in the World: Selected Papers of Ludwig Binswanger*. (J. Needleman, Trans.) London: Souvenir Press.

Bonafoux, P. (1985). *Portraits of the Artist: The Self-Portrait in Painting*. New York: Skira/ Rizzoli International Publications, Inc.

Borges, J. L. (1981). In E. Monegal and A. Reid (Eds.), *Borges, A Reader*. New York: E. P. Dutton.

Bruner, J. (1986). *Actual Minds, Possible Worlds*. Cambridge: Harvard University Press.

Brunswick, R. M. (1928). A supplement to Freud's "History of an Infantile Neurosis." In M. Gardiner (Ed.), *The Wolf Man*. New York: Basic Books, 1971.

Buber, M. (1957). Elements of the interhuman. *Psychiatry*, 20: 105–113.

Buie, D. H. (1981). Empathy: its nature and limitations. *Journal of the American Psychoanalytic Association*, 29: 281–307.

Buie, D. H. (1984). Discussion of "Empathy: critical reevaluation" by T. Shapiro. In J. Lichtenberg, M. Bornstein, & D. Silver (Eds.), *Empathy I*. Hillsdale, New Jersey: The Analytic Press.

Deutsch, H. (1942). Some forms of emotional disturbances and their relationship to schizophrenia. *Psychoanalytic Quarterly*, 11: 301–321.

Edwards, B. (1979). *Drawing on the Right Side of the Brain*. Los Angeles: J. P. Tarcher, Inc.

Ellenberger, H. E. (1970). *The Discovery of the Unconscious: The History and Evolution of Dynamic Psychiatry*. New York: Basic Books.

Ellenberger, H. F. (1958). A clinical introduction to psychiatric phenomenology and existential analysis. In R. May, E. Angel, & H. F. Ellenberger (Eds.), *Existence*. New York: Simon and Schuster.

Engell, J. (1981). *The Creative Imagination: Enlightenment to Romanticism*. Cambridge: Harvard University Press.

Erikson, E. H. (1954). The dream specimen of psychoanalysis. *The Journal of the American Psychoanalytic Association*, 2: 5–56.

Flam, J. (1978). *Matisse on Art*. New York: E. P. Dutton.

Freedman, A. M., Kaplan, H. I., & Sadock, B. J. (1975). *Comprehensive Textbook of Psychiatry-II*, Vol. II. Baltimore: Williams & Wilkins Co.

Freud, S. (1900). The interpretation of dreams. *Standard Edition* 4, 5. New York: Norton, 1953.

Freud, S. (1904). Freud's psycho-analytic procedure. *Standard Edition* 7: 249–254. New York: Norton, 1953.

Freud, S. (1909). Notes upon a case of obsessional neurosis. *Standard Edition* 10: 151–318. New York: Norton, 1955.

Freud, S. (1911). Psycho-analytic notes on an autobiographical account of a case of paranoia (demential paranoides). *Standard Edition* 12: 1–79. New York: Norton, 1958.

Freud, S. (1912). Recommendations to physicians practicing psycho-analysis. *Standard Edition* 12: 109–120. New York: Norton, 1958.

Freud, S. (1913). On beginning the treatment (Further recommendations on the technique of psycho-analysis I). *Standard Edition* 12: 123–144. New York: Norton, 1958.

Freud, S. (1915–16). Introductory lectures on psycho-analysis. *Standard Edition* 15: 1–79. New York: Norton, 1961.

Freud, S. (1917). Mourning and melancholia. *Standard Edition* 14: 237–258. New York: Norton, 1957.

Freud, S. (1921). Group psychology and the analysis of the ego. *Standard Edition*. 18: 65–144. New York: Norton, 1955.

Freud, S. (1923a). Two encyclopaedia articles. *Standard Edition* 18: 235–262. New York: Norton, 1955.

Freud, S. (1923b). The ego and the id. *Standard Edition* 19: 1–66. New York: Norton, 1961.

Freud, S. (1930). Civilization and its discontents. *Standard Edition* 21: 57–146. New York: Norton, 1961.

Freud, S. (1933). New introductory lectures on psycho-analysis. *Standard Edition* 22: 1–182. New York: Norton, 1964.

Freud, S. (1940). An outline of psychoanalysis. *Standard Edition* 23: 139–208. New York: Norton, 1964.

Freud, S. (1954). In M. Bonaparte, A. Freud, & E. Kris, (Eds.), *The Origins of Psychoanalysis: Letters to Wilhelm Fliess, Drafts and Notes: 1887–1902*. (E. Mosbacher & J. Strachey, Trans.). New York: Basic Books, Inc.

Gardner, H. (1985). *The Mind's New Science: A History of the Cognitive Revolution*. New York: Basic Books.

Gardner, M. R. (1983). *Self-Inquiry*. New York: Little, Brown & Company.

Gazzaniga, M. (1985). *The Social Brain: Discovering the Networks of the Mind*. New York: Basic Books.

Von Gebsattel, V. E. (1938). The world of the compulsive. In R. May, E. Angel, & H. F. Ellenberger (Eds.), *Existence*. New York: Basic Books, 1958.

Gilligan, C. (1982). *In A Different Voice: Psychological Theory and Women's Development*. Cambridge: Harvard University Press.

Griffith, J., Cavanaugh, J., Held, J., Oates, J. (1972). Dextroamphetamine: evaluation of psychomimetic properties in man. *Archives of General Psychiatry*, 26: 97–100.

Grossman, W. I. (1982). The self as fantasy: fantasy as theory. *Journal of the American Psychoanalytic Association*, 30: 919–937.

Grotstein, J. S. (1984). Some perspectives on empathy from others and toward oneself. In J. Lichtenberg, M. Bornstein, D. Silver (Eds.), *Empathy I*. Hillsdale, New Jersey: The Analytic Press.

Grunebaum, H. and Perlman, M. (1973). Paranoia and naivete: Coexisting traits in three patients. *Archives of General Psychiatry*, 28: 30–32.

Gustafson, J. P. (1986). *The Complex Secret of Brief Psychotherapy*. New York: Norton.

Hanly, C. M. (1979). *Existentialism and Psychoanalysis*. New York: International Universities Press, Inc.

Harlow, H. F. (1958). The nature of love. *American Psychologist*, 12: 673–685.

Havens, L. L. (1962). The placement and movement of hallucinations in space: Phenomenology and theory. *International Journal of Psychoanalysis*, 43: 426–435.

Havens, L. L. (1973). *Approaches to the Mind, Movement of the Psychiatric Schools from Sects toward Science*. Boston: Little, Brown and Company.

Havens, L. L. (1974). The existential use of the self. *American Journal of Psychiatry*, 131: 1–10.

Havens, L. L. (1976). *Participant Observation*. New York: Jason Aronson.

Havens, L. L. (1978a). Explorations in the uses of language in psychotherapy: Simple empathic statements. *Psychiatry*, 41: 336–345.

Havens, L. L. (1978b). Explorations in the use of language in psychotherapy: Complex empathic statements. *Psychiatry*, 42: 40–48.

Havens, L. L. (1984a). Explorations in the uses of language in psychotherapy: Counterintrojective statements (performatives). *Contemporary Psychoanalysis*, 20: 385–399.

Havens, L. L. (1986). *Making Contact, Uses of Language in Psychotherapy*. Cambridge: Harvard University Press.

Havens, L. L. (1989). *The Human Ground*. (In preparation).

Hofstadter, D. R. (1979). *Gödel, Escher, Bach: An Eternal Golden Braid*. New York: Basic Books.

Horney, K. (1937). *The Neurotic Personality of Our Time*. New York: Norton.

Horney, K. (1939). *New Ways in Psychoanalysis*. New York: Norton.

Horney, K. (1945). *Our Inner Conflicts*. New York: Norton.

Horney, K. (1950). *Neurosis and Human Growth: The Struggle Toward Self-Realization*. New York: Norton.

Horowitz, M. J. (1983). *Image Formation and Psychotherapy*. New York: Jason Aronson, Inc.

Husserl, E. (1962). *Ideas, General Introduction to Pure Phenomenology*. (W. R. Gibson, Trans). New York: Collier Books.

Ihde, D. (1977). *Experimental Phenomenology*. New York: G. P. Putnam's Sons.

Jacobs, T. (1986). Transference relationships, the relationships between transference, and reconstruction. Presentation to the American Psychoanalytic Association Annual Meeting, May 1986.

Jacobson, E. (1957). Denial and repression. *Journal of the American Psychoanalytic Association*, 5: 61–92.

Janowsky, D., El-Yousef, M., Davis, J., & Sekerke, H. (1973). Provocation of schizophrenic symptoms by intravenous administration of methylphenidate. *Archives of General Psychiatry*, 28: 185–191.

Johnson-Laird, P. (1983). *Mental Models*. Cambridge: Harvard University Press.

Jung, C. G. (1934). The practical use of dream analysis. In C. G. Jung, *Dreams*. (R. F. C. Hull, Trans.) Princeton: Princeton University Press, 1974.

Jung, C. G. (1965). In A. Jaffé (Ed.), *Memories, Dreams, Reflections*. (R. and C. Winston, Trans.). New York: Random House.

Jung, C. G. (1952). Individual dream symbolism in relation to alchemy. In C. G. Jung, *Dreams*. (R. F. C. Hull, Trans.) Princeton: Princeton University Press, 1974.

Keats, J. (1958). In H. E. Rollins (Ed.), *The Letters of John Keats, Vol. I*. Cambridge: Harvard University Press.

Khantzian, E. J. (1988). Affects and addictive suffering: A clinical perspective. Unpublished manuscript.

Kline, N. and Rausch, J. (1985). Olfactory precipitants of flashbacks in posttraumatic stress disorder: Case reports. *The Journal of Clinical Psychiatry*, 46: 383–384.

Klüver, H. (1966). *Mescal and Mechanisms of Hallucinations*. Chicago: The University of Chicago Press.

Kohák, E. (1978). *Idea and Experience: Edmund Husserl's Project of Phenomenology in Ideas I*. Chicago: The University of Chicago Press.

Kohut, H. (1971). *The Analysis of the Self*. New York: International Universities Press.

Kohut, H. (1977). *The Restoration of the Self*. New York: International Universities Press.

Kohut, H. (1984). *How Does Analysis Cure?* Chicago: University of Chicago Press.

Kris, E. (1952). *Psychoanalytic Explorations in Art*. New York: International Universities Press.

Kris, E. (1956). The personal myth: A problem in psychoanalytic technique. *Journal of the American Psychoanalytic Association*, 4: 653–681.

Kundera, M. (1988). *The Art of the Novel*. (L. Asher, Trans.) New York: Grove Press.

Langfeld, H. S. (1920). *The Aesthetic Attitude*. New York: Harcourt, Brace and Howe.

Langs, R. (1975). Therapeutic misalliances. *International Journal of Psychoanalytic Psychotherapy*, 4: 77–105.

Laplanche, J. & Pontalis, J.-B. (1973). *The Language of Psycho-Analysis*. (D. Nicholson-Smith, Trans.) New York: W. W. Norton & Co.

Leavy, S. A. (1970). John Keats's psychology of creative imagination. *The Psychoanalytic Quarterly*, 39: 173–197.

Leder, D. (1987). Toward a phenomenology of pain. *Review of Existential Psychology & Psychiatry*. Vol 19: 255–266.

Lem, S. (1968). *His Master's Voice*. (M. Kandel, Trans.) New York: Harcourt, Brace, Jovanovich.

Luria, A. R. (1968). *The Mind of a Mnemonist*. (L. Solotaroff, Trans.) New York: Avon Books.

MacKenzie, N. H. (1981). *A Reader's Guide to Gerard Manley Hopkins*. New York: Cornell University Press.

Margulies, A. (1984). Toward empathy: The uses of wonder. *American Journal of Psychiatry*, 141: 1025–1033.

Margulies, A. (1985). On listening to a dream: The sensory dimensions. *Psychiatry*, 48: 371–381.

Margulies, A. & Havens, L. (1981). The initial encounter: What to do first? *American Journal of Psychiatry*, 138: 421–428.

May, R. (1958). Contributions of existential psychotherapy. In R. May, E. Angel & H. F. Ellenberger (Eds.), *Existence*. New York: Simon and Schuster.

May, R. (1969). The emergence of existential psychology. In R. May (Ed.), *Existential Psychology*. New York: Random House.

Meares, R. (1983). Keats and the impersonal therapist: A note on empathy and the therapeutic screen. *Psychiatry*, 46: 73–82.

Merleau-Ponty, M. (1964). In J. Edie (Ed.), *The Primacy of Perception*. Chicago: Northwestern University Press.

Merleau-Ponty, M. (1964). What is phenomenology? In M. Friedman (Ed.), The Worlds of Existentialism. Chicago: The University of Chicago Press.

Minkowski, E. (1970). *Lived Time: Phenomenological and Psychopathological Studies*. (N. Metzel, Transl.) Chicago: Northwestern University Press.

Minsky, M. (1985). *The Society of Mind*. New York: Simon and Schuster.

Moore, B. E., and Fine, B. D. (1968). *A Glossary of Psychoanalytic Terms and Concepts*. New York: The American Psychoanalytic Association.

Misiak, H. & Sexton, V. S. (1973). *Phenomenological, Existential and Humanistic Psychologies*: A Historical Survey. New York: Grune & Stratton.

Nagel, T. (1974). What is it like to be a bat? In D. Hofstadter & D. Dennett (Eds.), *The Mind's I: Fantasies and Reflections on Self & Soul*. New York, Basic Books, 1981.

Nemiah, J. (1984). Anxiety and psychodynamic theory. In L. Grinspoon (Ed.), *Psychiatry Update*, Vol III. Washington, D.C.: Psychiatric Press.

Niederland, W. G. (1959a). The 'miracled -up' world of Schreber's childhood. *Psychoanalytic Study of the Child*, 14: 383–413.

Niederland, W. G. (1959b). Schreber: father and son. *Psychoanalytic Quarterly*, 28: 151–169.

Penfield, W. (1975). *The Mystery of the Mind: A Critical Study of Consciousness and the Human Brain*. New Jersey: Princeton University Press.

Piaget, J. (1986). *The Construction of Reality in the Child*. (M. Cook, Trans.) New York: Ballantine.

Piaget, J. (1966). *The Origins of Intelligence in Children*. (M. Cook, Trans.) New York: International Universities Press.

Popper, K. (1968). *The Logic of Scientific Discovery*. New York: Harper & Row.

Proust, M. (1928). *Remembrance of Things Past*. (C. K. C. Moncrieff, Trans.) New York: Random House (1970).

Proust, M. (1981). *Remembrance of Things Past*. (C. K. C. Moncrieff and T. Kilmartin, Trans.) New York: Random House.

Rako, S. & Mazer, H. (1980). *Semrad: The Heart of a Therapist*. New York: Jason Aronson.

Rank, O. (1924). *The Trauma of Birth*. New York: Harcourt, Brace and Company, 1929.

Ricoeur, O. (1970). *Freud and Philosophy: An Essay on Interpretation*. (D. Savage, Trans.) New Haven: Yale University Press.

Rogers, C. (1965). *Client-Centered Therapy*. Boston: Houghton-Mifflin.

Roth, S. (1987). The practice of psychiatry and psychotherapy. Presentation at the 75th Anniversary of Massachusetts Mental Health Center, Harvard Medical School.

Rumelhart, D. E. (1975). Notes on a schema for stories. In D. Bobrow and A. Collins (Eds.), *Representation and Understanding: Studies in Cognitive Science*. New York: Academic Press.

Ryle, G. (1950). *The Concept of Mind*. New York: Barnes & Noble, Inc.

Sandler, J. (1976). Countertransference and role responsiveness. *International Review of Psycho-Analysis*, 3: 43–47.

Sartre, J. P. (1956). *Being and Nothingness: An Essay on Phenomenological Ontology*. (H. E. Barnes, Trans). New York: Philosophical Library.

Sashin, J. I. (1985). Affect tolerance: A model of affect-response using catastrophe theory. *J. Social Biol. Struct.*, 8: 175–202

Schwaber, E. (1981). Empathy: a mode of analytic listening. *Psychoanalytic Inquiry*, 1: 357–392.

Schwaber, E. (1983). Psychoanalytic listening and psychic reality. *International Review of Psychoanalysis*, 10: 379–392.

Schwaber, E. (1984). Response to: "On seeing things; some reflections on the analyzing instrument" by M. Robert Gardner. Presented at Scientific Meeting of the Psychoanalytic Institute of New England, East, Jan. 15, 1984.

Schwaber, E. (1986). Reconstruction and perceptual experience: further thoughts on psychoanalytic listening. *Journal of the American Psychoanalytic Association*, 34: 911–932.

Semrad, E. V., Grinspoon, L. & Feinberg, S. E. (1973). Development of an ego profile scale. *Archives of General Psychiatry*, 28: 70–77.

Shapiro, D. (1965). *Neurotic Styles*. New York: Basic Books.

Sherwood, M. (1969). *The Logic of Explanation in Psychoanalysis*. New York: Academic Press.

Sifneos, P. E. (1972). *Short-Term Psychotherapy and Emotional Crisis*. Cambridge: Harvard University Press.

Sloane, P. (1979). *Psychoanalytic Understanding of the Dream*. Jason Aronson.

Spence, D. P. (1982). *Narrative Truth and Historical Truth: Meaning and Interpretation in Psychoanalysis*. New York: Norton.

Stern, D. (1985). *The Interpersonal World of the Infant*. New York, Basic Books.

Strachey, J. & Strachey, A. (1985). In P. Miesel and W. Kendrick (Eds.), *Bloomsbury/Freud: The Letters of James and Alix Strachey, 1924-1925*. New York: Basic Books.

Straus, E. W. (1948). Aesthesiology and Hallucinations. In R. May, E. Angel, & H. F. Ellenberger (Eds.), *Existence*, New York: Basic Books, 1958.

Straus, E. W. (1966). *Phenomenological Psychology: Selected Papers*. (E. Eng, Trans.) New York: Basic Books.

Sullivan, H. S. (1953a). *Conceptions of Modern Psychiatry*. New York: Norton.

Sullivan, H. S. (1953b). *The Interpersonal Theory of Psychiatry*. New York: Norton.

Sullivan, H. S. (1954). *The Psychiatric Interview*. New York: Norton.

Sullivan, H. S. (1956). *Clinical Studies in Psychiatry*. New York: Norton.

Süskind, P. (1986). *Perfume: The Story of a Murderer* (J. E. Woods, Trans.). New York: Alfred A. Knopf.

Vaillant, G. E. (1976). Natural history of male psychological health: V. The relation of choice of ego mechanisms of defense to adult adjustment. *Archives of General Psychiatry*, 33: 535-545.

Vaillant, G. E. (1977). *Adaptation to Life*. Boston: Little, Brown and Company.

Viderman, S. 1979. The analytic space: meaning and problems. *Psychoanalytic Quarterly*, 48: 257-91.

Waelder, R. (1962). Psychoanalysis, scientific method, and philosophy. *Journal of the American Psychoanalytic Association*, 10: 617-637.

Wolff, P. H. (1966a). The causes, controls and organization of behavior in the neonate. *Psychological Issues*, 5: 17.

Wolff, P. H. (1966b). The real and the reconstructed past: comments on the relation of infant observations to psychoanalytic reconstruction. Presented at Scientific Meeting of the Boston Psychoanalytic Society and Institute, Nov. 30, 1966.

Wyss, D. (1973). *Psychoanalytic Schools from the Beginning to the Present*. New York: Jason Aronson.

Yalom, I. D. (1980). *Existential Psychotherapy*. New York: Basic Books.

Zetzel, E. & Meissner, W. W. (1973). *Basic Concepts of Psychoanalytic Psychiatry*. New York: Basic Books.

Acknowledgments

E very now and then it takes me by surprise. The term is "thrownness," that is, the extraordinary uniqueness of one's personal life's circumstances, the context into which one is born — thrown — by the dice of existence. And this is my own sometimes experience. Despite the inevitable heartbreak in every life, by any measure of luck I have been unusually fortunate, cast into my own unrepeatable circumstances. A life is made up of the particulars, the texture of context and situation. And I have chanced to meet remarkable people along the way. This book is surely a reflection of that good fortune. To convey properly the important influences on it, I would need to write an autobiography. Here I will thank those most immediate to this book.

Elvin Semrad and Marilyn Powers, both now gone, had an immense influence early on in my life as a student. Semrad made empathy the center of therapeutic work. Marilyn, a painter, brought an extraordinary integrity and passion to seeing things freshly. I see more clearly now how similar they were.

After many years of friendship Leston Havens never ceases to surprise me with the originality and freedom of his thinking. He has served as mentor, colleague, and friend with remarkable patience and faith—he has truly been there for me. His ideas are the foundation for many of my own.

Colleagues at the Psychoanalytic Institute of New England have been extremely receptive to my work, and I am grateful. Sheldon Roth, with his characteristic warmth, wisdom, and directness, offered me careful readings of the manuscript. Evelyne Albrecht Schwaber has been encouraging throughout the life of the book, and I have learned much from her clinical sensitivity and empathic subtlety; anyone familiar with her work will recognize her influence on my own. Samuel Silverman, too, set an example in his steady, experienced clinical awareness; Frances Bonner in her warm and intuitive brilliance.

At The Cambridge Hospital, Myron Belfer has provided a setting for me to grow. As Chairman of the department of psychiatry, he holds together a remarkably diverse group of people in the hectic arena of public sector psychiatry.

Among my colleagues and friends, several have wrestled with my writings and have provided invaluable help: John Mack, Paul Erickson, Carol Daynard, Richard Daynard, Joseph Glenmullen, Pat Carr, Bruce Gage, Joseph Loizzo, Alice Flaherty, Richard Goldstein, Christopher Wallis, Edward Emery, Jerome Sashin, Myron Sharaf, James Gustafson, and Bennett Simon. Susan Barrows, my editor, sought me out, setting off a series of events that I never imagined. Though I initially rejected the idea of a book, I came back to it. For her, it must have been like feeding a squirrel; she had the patience to know how.

A family provides the warmth, stimulation, and loving tension of everyday existence. If ever there was a confirmation of the interpersonal dialectical spiral, it is to be found in the intimacy of our private relationships. Bonnie, as wife and confidante, keeps me down to earth and yet buoys me up. She more than anyone else has struggled with me to the realization of the ideas presented here. My children, Lauren and Lisa, have taught me a great deal about living, loving, and implicit acceptance; what you give you receive back manifold.

Lastly, I must add a word about my use of clinical material. Anyone who has faced the plight of publishing studies about the process of psychotherapy knows what a difficult and vexing problem the question of confidentiality is. One is obligated ethically to disguise the material presented in such a fashion that it becomes unrecognizable to those outside of the process. This renders the material virtually useless to other researchers and prevents the inclusion of some of the everyday minutiae that comprises the distinct feel of a life and its unique world view. Freud, struggling over the same concerns, wrote (1909, p. 156): " . . . it is far easier to divulge the patient's most intimate secrets than the most innocent and trivial facts about him; for, whereas the former would not throw any light on his identity, the latter, by which he is generally recognized, would make it obvious to every one." The cases I present are heavily disguised. Nevertheless, I have tried to remain true to the process and the experience. I owe a debt of gratitude to those who have shared their lives with me, and who must remain anonymous.

To all of you, thank you — I would not have been me without you.

Index

regression in the service of the ego, 13
repetition compulsion:
  and character, 94
  and compulsivity as centering, 100–1
  and inertia of world view, 85, 91–94
  and interpersonal matrix, 91–92, 93–94
  as *raison d'etre*, 101–6
  theoretical conceptualizations of, 91–92
Ricoeur, P., 11, 12
Rogers, C., 13, 18
Roth, S., 30, 81–82
Rumelhart, D. E., 149*n*
Ryle, G., 138, 139

Sadock, B. J., 4, 7
Sandler, J., 92, 118
Sartre, J. P., 31, 102, 137
Sashin, J. I., 131, 148*n*, 150*n*
Schwaber, E., 76, 129, 160
secret:
  pathogenic, 68, 119, 150
  as protected life's passion, 96
Sekerke, H., 89
self:
  as archetype, 136
  as a "category mistake" of language, 138
  and its center, 137–39
  cultural context, 127
  defined through the other, 103–6
  discontinuous, 129–32
  as ego, 116
  as the enemy, 120
  existential formulations, 137–39
  as gerund, 117, 139–40
  as homunculus, 136
  and internalized/externalized objects, 137
  interpersonal formulations, 137–39
  and layers of the mind, 135
  naming the self, 133–35
  narrative (self as story), 109, 117, 139
  as noun, 133–39
  as personal myth, 117, 139
  of the poet (Keats), 14
  as possibility, 128, 130–31, 142
  as process, 116–17, 139–43
  and paradox as an essence of, 108–9,
    125, 132–33, 140–43
  self-objectifying-the-self, 9–10
  the self-reflective interpersonal spiral, 107
  and self-revision, 110–12, 117
  as society of selves, 138
  and spatial metaphors, 135–39
  as subject and object, 109
  as theoretical fiction, 138
  from theoretical perspectives, 138–39
  as unnameable, 135
  as verb, 139
  as world view, 126
  see also empathy with self; me/not-me; self-recursive self
self-recursive self, 34, 98, 140–43
  as broken and dying, 140–43
  and finding oneself through the other, 109–10
  self-observing-self, 110
  see also recursion; empathy with self
self-reflective interpersonal spiral, 77, 99, 107, 114–17, 133
  as broken, 140–43
  and creation of possibilities, 130–31
  stymied, 119–25
  see also empathy with oneself; recursion; recursive ego; self-recursive self
self-soothing, 65
selfobject, 110, 130, 137
  disruption of ties, 75–76
  feminist contributions, 151*n*
Semrad, E. V., 16–17, 93, 106, 128, 131, 136, 151*n*
sensory dimensions, 21–34
  see also specific modalities
Sexton, V. S., 9
Shakespeare, W., 16, 28
Shapiro, D., 87
Sherwood, M., 117, 139
Sifneos, P. E., 44
sight and activity, 30
Simon, B., 150*n*
Sloane, P., 31
"Social Brain," and "Society of Mind," 138
sound, 25
  receptivity and helplessness, 30
  unique relation to time, 25–28